From Ragtime to Hip-Hop:
A Century of Black American Music

Lucent Library of Black History

Adam Woog

LUCENT BOOKS

An imprint of Thomson Gale, a part of The Thomson Corporation

Detroit • New York • San Francisco • New Haven, Conn. • Waterville, Maine • London

This one's for the other Friday Lunch Boys—Tom DeGraff, Ross Reynolds, and Bob Rini—with thanks and appreciation for their always stimulating discussions about music and other vital subjects.

On cover: Kanye West performs at a concert in Los Angeles in 2005.

LIBRARY OF CONGRESS CATALOGING-IN-PUBLICATION DATA

Woog, Adam, 1953–
From ragtime to hip-hop : a century of Black American music / by Adam Woog.
        p. cm. — (Lucent library of Black history)
Includes bibliographical references and index.
ISBN-13: 978-1-59018-978-8 (hardcover : alk. paper)
ISBN-10: 1-59018-978-7 (hardcover : alk. paper)
1. African Americans—Music—History and criticism—Juvenile literature.   2. Popular music—United States—History and criticism—Juvenile literature.   I. Title.
ML3556.W68 2005
781.64089'96073—dc22
                                                                              2006019960

Printed in the United States of America

Contents

Foreword

It has been more than five hundred years since Africans were first brought to the New World in shackles, and over 140 years since slavery was formally abolished in the United States. Over 50 years have passed since the fallacy of "separate but equal" was obliterated in the American courts, and some forty years since the watershed Civil Rights Act of 1965 guaranteed the rights and liberties of all Americans, especially those of color. Over time, these changes have become celebrated landmarks in American history. In the twenty-first century, African American men and women are politicians, judges, diplomats, professors, deans, doctors, artists, athletes, business owners, and home owners. For many, the scars of the past have melted away in the opportunities that have been found in contemporary society. Observers such as Peter N. Kirsanow, who sits on the U.S. Commission of Civil Rights, point to these accomplishments and conclude, "The growing black middle class may be viewed as proof that most of the civil rights battles have been won."

In spite of these legal victories, however, prejudice and inequality have persisted in American society. In 2003, African Americans comprised just 12 percent of the nation's population, yet accounted for 44 percent of its prison inmates and 24 percent of its poor. Racially motivated hate crimes continue to appear on the pages of major newspapers in many American cities. Furthermore, many African Americans still experience either overt or muted racism in their daily lives. A 1996 study undertaken by Professor Nancy Krieger of the Harvard School of Public Health, for example, found that 80 percent of the African American participants reported having experienced racial discrimination in one or more settings, including at work or school, applying for housing and medical care, from the police or in the courts, and on the street or in a public setting.

It is for these reasons that many believe the struggle for racial equality and justice is far from over. These episodes of discrimination threaten to shatter the illusion that America has completely overcome its racist past, causing many black Americans to become increasingly frustrated and confused. Scholar and writer Ellis Cose has described this splintered state in the following way: "I have done everything I was supposed to do. I have stayed out of trouble with the law, gone to the right schools, and worked myself nearly to death. What more do they want? Why in God's name won't they accept me as a full human being?" For Cose and others, the struggle for equality and justice has yet to be fully achieved.

In many subtle yet important ways the traumatic experiences of slavery and segregation continue to inform the way race is discussed and experienced in the twenty-first century. Indeed, it is possible that America will always grapple with the fallout from its distressing past. Ulric Haynes, dean of the Hofstra University School of Business has said, "Perhaps race will always matter, given the historical circumstances under which we came to this country." But studying this past and understanding how it contributes to present-day dialogues about race and history in America is a critical component of contemporary education. To this end, the Lucent Library of Black History offers a thorough look at the experiences that have shaped the black community and the American people as a whole. Annotated bibliographies provide readers with ideas for further research, while fully documented primary and secondary source quotations enhance the text. Each book in the series explores a different episode of black history; together they provide students with a wealth of information as well as launching points for further study and discussion.

A Hundred Years—and More—of Music

Over the hundred-plus years of its history, black popular music in America has had many shapes and names: ragtime, gospel, swing, bebop, country blues, electric blues, rhythm and blues, soul, funk, new jack swing, nusoul, rap, hip-hop, and more. This diversity has provided, and still provides, a deep wellspring of styles from which to draw.

As it has evolved, black American music has come to dominate popular music. Once it was the overlooked pastime of an oppressed minority; today, it is the single most significant influence on all of American pop music—and, by extension, on world music as well. Without black musicians, there would be no rock and roll, no blues, no jazz, no soul or funk; nor would rap be the dominant genre of current American popular music.

Indeed, many observers feel that black popular music is the United States' greatest cultural achievement and its most precious gift to the world. Jazz trumpeter Wynton Marsalis comments, "The uniquely American legacy of swing and blues [is] a history to be valued, an artistic achievement that is on a par with the most magnificent works of Western classical music."[1]

"It's All *About* Feelings"

Marsalis mentions only two of black popular music's subgroups. These various genres have obvious differences but also frequently blend, with overlaps that make them tough to differentiate or neatly categorize. On the other hand, much of the fun of listening to music is spotting differences and common ground—discovering, for example, what separates or binds together blues and gospel.

Even casual listening reveals that, despite their differences, the varieties of black popular music have some basic elements in common. The most vital of these hark back to the musical traditions

Aretha Franklin, known as the Queen of Soul, performs a song on a 1975 television special.

Salvation vs. a Pit of Despair

◼

To deeply religious people, the differences separating gospel from jazz and blues were stark. They felt that the rhythms and melodies of jazz and blues were sinfully suggestive. They were also appalled by the message that this music sent. To them, jazz represented wanton wickedness, and the blues was the sound of despair. In contrast, spiritual music delivered a message of stability, hope, happiness, and love. As the legendary gospel singer Mahalia Jackson once commented, "Somebody singing blues is crying out of a pit. I'm singing out of the joy of my salvation."

Quoted in Anthony Heilbut, *The Gospel Sound: Good News and Bad Times.* New York: Limelight, 1997, p. 299.

of Africa. Such characteristics as complex rhythms and the use of blue notes are direct descendants of music brought to North America by slaves.

The subgenres of black music share another important characteristic as well: They all pack an emotional punch. The emotion might be sadness or happiness, anger or exhilaration, yearning or satisfaction—but it is always there. As Aretha Franklin, the Queen of Soul, once remarked: "It's all *about* feelings. You can't get away from that fact, no matter what you do."[2]

Into the Mainstream

African American music, like other types of music, has evolved over time, one style emerging from the preceding one. Music, in this sense, resembles slowly evolving life. But changes can also be startlingly fast.

A major change in black pop music occurred as the nineteenth century ended and the twentieth century began. Before then, the music was a folk style, encompassing both religious and nonreligious songs, generally known only to black audiences. Widespread, mass audiences—which is to say, white audiences—knew it only through a form of entertainment called minstrel shows.

Within a few decades, however, three major genres—jazz, blues, and gospel—developed and attracted a wide audience. This began the process of black music breaking into the American musical mainstream.

Over the next decades, jazz, blues, and gospel evolved within their own boundaries. The hot jazz of the early twentieth century, for instance, morphed into a style called swing; this happened so quickly that *Downbeat* magazine noted, "In the early thirties swing was creeping up on the American citizen, and in 1935 it struck him so forcibly that he didn't know what happened."[3] Swing, in turn, quickly went out of fashion to make way for the next major jazz style.

In its earliest years, however, African American music did not change that quickly; at any rate, few records document such changes. During the slave era, black popular music was simply what slaves sang, and it was mostly ignored by those in a position to document it—the white slaveholders. But enough writing does exist from that time to provide a rough idea of these roots of black music.

Chapter One

The Roots of Black Music

The first slaves arrived in North America from Africa in the early 1600s. By 1750, an estimated two hundred thousand were in the colonies. They worked primarily in the South, where massive numbers were needed for such labor-intensive crops as rice, tobacco, and cotton.

Slaves had no civil rights. They were bought and sold like cattle; lived in wretched conditions; and were routinely beaten, raped, and separated from their families. The slaves had few comforts, but at least they had music. Music helped them retain some solace and a bit of their African identity, even in the face of inhuman punishment.

African Music

The slaves came from several distinct groups. Their music thus reflected different cultures. Broadly speaking, however, it shared certain characteristics.

For example, vocal music was typically group singing. Generally, a solo vocalist alternated with an answering chorus, a style today called call-and-response. Another shared element was the use of certain scales, such as the five-note pentatonic scale, and flatted notes, which today are called bent or blue notes.

A third major characteristic of African music was the use of polyrhythms—multiple, overlapping rhythms, such as 4/4 (four beats to a measure) played against 3/4 (three beats to a measure, or waltz time). These rhythms were played on drums, with sticks, and with body percussion such as hand claps.

These main characteristics of African music—call-and-response singing, certain scales and notes, and polyrhythms—would, in time, form the foundation of American black music. Indeed, they would influence music all over the world. Music historian Robert Darden comments: "Among the richest of the lavish gifts Africa has given the world is rhythm. The beat. The sound of wood on wood, hand on hand."[4]

Songs

In Africa, singing, dancing, and drumming were crucial parts of life. Daily occurrences and major events alike were commemorated

Slaves pick cotton on a plantation in the 1850s. The vocals of slave songs were usually improvised.

"Every Tone Was a Testimony"

■

Spirituals inspired hope, asked for forgiveness and freedom, and affirmed a deep faith in a better life. African American leader Frederick Douglass, remembering a childhood spent in slavery, wrote about them: "They told a tale which was then altogether beyond my feeble comprehension; they were tones, loud, long, and deep, breathing the prayer and complaint of souls boiling over with the bitterest anguish. Every tone was a testimony against slavery, and a prayer to God for deliverance from chains."

Quoted in Bernice Johnson Reagon, ed., *We'll Understand It Better By and By: Pioneering African American Gospel Composers*. Washington, DC: Smithsonian Institution, 1992, p. 11.

with song. Historian Eileen Southern writes, "For almost every activity in the life of the individual or the community there was an appropriate music; it was an integral part of life from the hour of birth to beyond the grave."[5]

Slaves did their best to reproduce familiar music. They made instruments with materials at hand, such as flutes made from lengths of cane. Occasionally, they also learned new styles; whites sometimes taught slaves to play Western instruments such as the violin.

But slaves usually were forbidden to play drums. In Africa, drummers could use their instruments to communicate over distances. By banning drums, slave masters kept slaves on isolated plantations from planning rebellions with others.

Despite this restriction, slaves always had one instrument with them: the voice. And so they sang. As new generations grew up and old African languages were forgotten, the songs of the slaves were increasingly in English.

These songs reflected the African tradition of improvisation. African singers routinely put individual stamps on even familiar songs, and slaves continued to use the technique. They altered old melodies and lyrics or invented entirely new songs. This sharply contrasted with European folk music traditions, which emphasized exact reproduction.

12

The slaves sang for many reasons. A song might be a lullaby, a work song, a mournful complaint, or a tune sung simply for pleasure. Sometimes this pleasure involved making fun of owners; an observer in Maryland noted in 1774 that slaves amused themselves when at rest with "very droll music indeed," singing lyrics about their masters and mistresses "in a very satirical manner."[6]

Religious Song

Another important reason for singing was to express religious faith. The first slaves brought African religion with them, but slaves were also introduced to the Christianity of their masters.

Although in some cases Christianity was forced on slaves, most embraced it wholeheartedly. Christianity's promise of an afterlife offered hope, and its declaration of the equality of people before God appealed to slaves. Furthermore, the Bible's simple, powerful stories—of Moses delivering the Jews from bondage, of Jonah regaining freedom through faith—resonated powerfully.

During worship services, the races were generally kept separate, although sometimes they were allowed to mingle. For example, camp meetings—open-air occasions for preaching and singing—had both black and white congregations. A Swedish visitor attending a meeting in Georgia in the early 1800s noted: "A magnificent choir! Most likely the sound proceeded from the black portion of the assembly, as their number was three times that of the whites, and their voices are naturally beautiful and pure."[7]

Over time, African religious music merged with its European counterpart. From this mixture, a large, varied, and anonymously written body of songs developed. Songs once sung to ancestors or African gods were now sung to Jesus or Moses. Such songs eventually became known as spirituals. These powerful reflections of slave life were, in the words of the African American composer James Weldon Johnson, "forged of sorrow in the heat of religious fervor."[8]

Spirituals

Slaves radically changed the solemn, slow, and gloomy European hymns of the time. They embellished melodies with blue notes, bent notes, or melisma, a technique in which one syllable is

A group of slaves sings together. The lyrics of some slave songs provided directions along the Underground Railroad.

stretched over several notes. They also added polyrhythms or freely changed lyrics.

The lyrics of spirituals frequently had double meanings, with images that evoked both religious salvation and freedom from slavery. Some double meanings held coded messages associated with the Underground Railroad, the network of whites and free blacks that helped Southern slaves escape their bondage. In "Follow the Drinking Gourd," a famous example, the drinking gourd was the Big Dipper, and the song told escapees to maintain a northward course toward freedom:

The river ends between two hills

Follow the drinking gourd

There's another river on the other side

Follow the drinking gourd.[9]

Slavery Ends, New Churches Begin

"Follow the Drinking Gourd" was just one symbol of how slavery deeply divided the nation. All Northern states had abolished it by

1804, but the practice flourished throughout the South. The issue came to a head when the Southern states one by one seceded from the Union and the Civil War broke out in 1860.

When the South was defeated in that bloody conflict in 1865, slavery ended throughout the United States. Millions of newly freed slaves suddenly needed to enter mainstream life. One result of this major societal upheaval was the need for formal churches —something that previously had been denied to the slaves.

The number of black churches across the South exploded, and each denomination could develop its own style of music. Black churches in rural areas tended toward boisterous, uninhibited, countrified singing and preaching. The music of urban congregations, such as the African Methodist Episcopal (AME) Church, was typically more sedate.

"Soon the Land Rang"

In this passage, Ella Sheppard, a member of the Fisk Jubilee Singers, reflects on her experiences singing spirituals:

> The slave songs . . . were associated with slavery and
> the dark past, and represented things to be forgotten.
> Then, too, they were sacred to our parents who used
> them in their religious worship and shouted over them.
> We finally grew willing to sing them privately, and sit-
> ting upon the floor . . . we practiced softly, learning
> from each other the songs of our fathers. We did not
> dream of ever using them in public. Had Mr. White [the
> music director of the Fisk Jubilee Singers] suggested
> such a thing, we certainly [would have] rebelled. After
> many months we began to appreciate the wonderful
> beauty and power of our song; but continued to sing in
> public the usual choruses, duets, solos, etc. Occasional-
> ly two or three slave songs were sung at the close of the
> concert. But the demand of the public changed this
> order. Soon the land rang with our slave songs.

Quoted in James Haskins, *Black Music in America*. New York: HarperCollins, 1987, pp. 27–29.

The Minstrel Era

Prior to the Civil War, Northern whites knew almost nothing about black music. What they did know came from minstrel shows. These were revues with dancers, musicians, comedians, and singers who darkened their faces with blackface makeup and wore clothes that caricatured African Americans. Most minstrel performers were white, though a handful were black—and some of these used blackface makeup as well.

Minstrel shows were broad parodies, meant to give white audiences an entertaining view of plantation life. They were wildly popular, and dozens of performing troupes regularly toured North America and Europe. Southern writes, "For more than four decades . . . minstrelsy was the most popular form of theatrical entertainment in the United States and, to the rest of the world, America's unique contribution to the stage."[10]

Minstrels Everywhere

───────■───────

The pervasiveness of minstrel shows in American culture was thorough during the peak years of their popularity and lingers to an extent even today. Writer Robert Cantwell comments:

> The visual and linguistic coinage of [minstrel shows has been] circulating in America for a century and a half in thousands of forms beyond the stage itself: in sheet music, songbook and magazine covers, panoramas, popular lithographs, postcards, bookjackets, scrapbooks, albums, catalogues, advertisements, product packaging, toys, as well as films, radio, television, folk festivals, and now even music videos. It is quite impossible even to think about "folklife" without recourse to the many motifs and images that descend from minstrelsy, which may be said to [be] inextricably bound up with questions of race and racial identity.

Robert Cantwell, *When We Were Good: The Folk Revival.* Cambridge, MA: Harvard University Press, 1996, p. 25.

From today's standpoint, minstrel shows seem crude and grotesquely racist. However, their importance in musical history cannot be ignored. Because they introduced black culture, albeit a false view of it, to mainstream white audiences, they were early instances of American pop music crossing racial and social barriers. Previously, whites had mostly listened to white music, blacks to black music; now, however, that was beginning to change.

"Oh, Dem Golden Slippers"

The minstrel shows acquainted audiences with several musical instruments with black origins. For instance, the bones were polished animal bones played as percussion. The banjo was a stringed instrument from Africa that, in time, became central to white folk music as well. The fiddle, long common to both white and black music, was another staple of the minstrel show.

Several types of song were associated with minstrelsy. Some were folk tunes well-known in the black community, such as "Jimmy Crack Corn." Others were variations of familiar white folk melodies like "Turkey in the Straw."

But professional songwriters wrote many minstrel songs that are still familiar today. Most of these composers were white, such as Stephen Foster, whose songs include "Camptown Races" and "My Old Kentucky Home." A handful were African American, such as James A. Bland, the originator of such classics as "Oh, Dem Golden Slippers" and "Carry Me Back to Old Virginny."

The Fisk Jubilee Singers

A major turning point in black music came in the 1870s with a dramatic surge of interest in spirituals among white northerners. A student troupe, the Fisk Jubilee Singers from Fisk University in Nashville, sparked this interest.

Organized as a fund-raising effort for the school, the Jubilee Singers first toured in 1871. Their performances of sentimental ballads and patriotic songs were skilled and dignified, but the singers were not well received until they added spirituals. The addition was suggested by the group's musical director, who was white, and the singers were at first reluctant; no former slave or child of a slave wanted to be reminded of that hated era.

However, the Fisk group discovered that spirituals—their rough edges smoothed by European elements such as piano accompaniment and classically styled harmonies—struck a responsive chord in audiences. The group became a sensation and triumphantly sang for cheering crowds, U.S. presidents, and European royalty.

Within a few years, they earned enough to build a six-story building that is still a centerpiece of Fisk University. Meanwhile, imitation groups sprang up to take advantage of the Jubilee Singers' popularity. There was also increased demand for spirituals in sheet music, the main method of disseminating music in the days before recordings and radio.

"He Was Bad, Jim"

Besides spirituals, another form of black popular music that developed in the late 1800s and early 1900s was the ballad, a form of secular (nonreligious) folk song. Black ballads were modeled on ancient British storytelling songs, part of the traditional music of many white settlers.

Black musicians, naturally, incorporated African rhythms and vocal styles into the ballad form. They also created new lyrics and story lines. Music historians Thomas L. Morgan and William Barlow write, "Black songsters supplanted the tragic lovers and natural-disaster victims of the white tradition with a pantheon of African American folk heroes, tricksters, and outlaws."[11]

A familiar example of the black folk ballad is "John Henry," about a legendary "steel-drivin' man" who worked himself to death on the railroad. Another is "Stagger Lee," about a famous killer who was, in the words of writer Julius Lester, "so bad that the flies wouldn't even fly around his head in the summertime, and snow wouldn't fall on his house in the winter. He was bad, jim."[12]

Pentecostalism

As the ballad form developed, African American religious music continued to undergo changes. One major shift was created by the rise of a new movement called Pentecostalism, also known as the Holiness or Sanctified Church, around the turn of the twentieth century.

Pentecostalism was hugely popular among both black and white Christians, and hundreds of denominations developed

The Jubilee Singers of Fisk University, pictured here in 1875, were a successful touring group.

within it. The largest of the black Pentecostal churches was the Church of God in Christ (COGIC). Founded in Mississippi in 1895, by the 1920s COGIC claimed a membership in the hundreds of thousands.

Pentecostal worship was notably noisier than older churches. Churchgoers regularly spoke out during services, encouraging the preacher or testifying to their own faith. Sometimes they shouted, fainted, or ran up and down the aisles as the Holy Spirit moved them.

This euphoric feeling applied to music as well. Pentecostal group singing was more passionate than that of older congregations, and many churches added percussion as well. Music historian Horace Clarence Boyer notes that Pentecostal services were typified by "forceful and jubilant singing, dramatic testimonies, hand clapping, foot stamping, and beating of drums, tambourines, and triangles (and pots, pans, and washboards when professional instruments were not available)."[13]

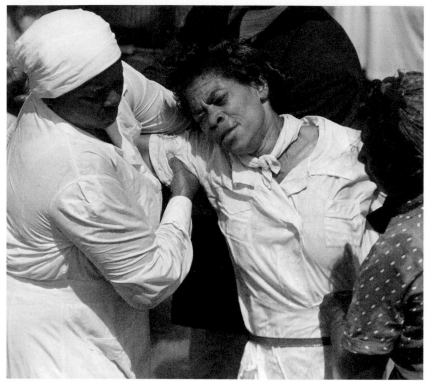

A woman overcome with emotion faints after her baptism at a Pentecostal church in Virginia in 1943.

Moving Northward

Though the Pentecostal movement was especially strong in rural areas, it also took root in cities. In part, this was because of a major shift in the nation's population during the early 1900s. During this period, huge numbers of people, including millions of African Americans, left their homes in the impoverished South for the industrialized cities of the Midwest and Northeast. The change was dramatic: In just the decade between 1910 and 1920, the black population of Chicago nearly doubled, while that of Detroit grew sixfold.

These immigrants, naturally, brought their music. During the next decades, black popular music flourished, developing into several key genres and moving steadily into mainstream American culture.

Chapter Two

Early Ragtime, Blues, and Jazz

Immigrants to the cities during the early twentieth century included the first generations of African Americans born after slavery. Among them—and among those who stayed in the South—were musicians who were beginning to develop three distinct but overlapping styles: ragtime, blues, and jazz.

In Rag Time

The term *ragtime* refers to a specific rhythmic style, syncopation, that occurs when a normally weak or unstressed beat is accented. Music historians David A. Jasen and Gene Jones call it "an ancient musical device, a trick that tickles the ear by putting a stress where we don't expect to hear it."[14]

The roots of ragtime were in the slave era. Slaves "ragged" European dance music by syncopating it on banjos and fiddles. The origin of the term is unclear, but one theory is that people fancifully imagined that the "cloth" of the music was becoming torn rags when it was syncopated.

Minstrel shows were quick to adopt this infectious blend of African rhythm and European song, performing music "in rag time." There were also many ragtime guitarists, such as Blind Blake. By the late 1800s, however, the piano was the instrument of choice.

The Popularity of Ragtime

In this passage, Thomas L. Morgan and William Barlow reflect on the reasons for ragtime's popularity:

> Ragtime's complex historical legacy was perhaps a major reason for its widespread appeal among both blacks and whites. First and foremost, it was a dance music which drew on both European and African traditions. Second, ragtime was a style grounded in an ongoing, cross-cultural, racial parody: the slaves' parody of their masters, blackface minstrels' trope of the blackface parody, and so on. In addition, ragtime was a rural folk music transposed to an urban and industrial context, where its machine-like rhythms became an expression of a lost innocence of bygone days and ways. And finally, as a novel popular music created by the first generation of African Americans born after slavery, ragtime represented an affirmation of their newly experienced freedoms and an optimistic vision of the future.

Thomas L. Morgan and William Barlow, *From Cakewalks to Concert Halls: An Illustrated History of African American Popular Music from 1895 to 1930*. Washington, DC: Elliott and Clark, 1992, p. 26.

As the United States grew more prosperous and settled, pianos became common in saloons, clubs, brothels, and middle-class homes. They proved ideal for ragtime's rhythms and harmonies. The left hand could pound out a steady beat while the right played intricate, syncopated melodies.

A number of professional musicians focused on ragtime during its formative years. The first published ragtime piece was "Michigan Waters," written in 1892 by Tony Jackson, a composer from New Orleans. The following year, Fred Stone, a Detroit musician, was the first to use the word *ragtime* in a song title: "Ma Ragtime Baby."

Cakewalking into Town

Ragtime pianists were especially popular in the red-light districts of midwestern and southern cities. Some were famous, such as

New Orleans' legendary Ferdinand "Jelly Roll" Morton. Others were forgotten despite having colorful names like Bad Hooks, Pluck Henry, Jack the Bear, and No Legs Cagey.

One man in particular became ragtime's most important figure. Scott Joplin, born in Texas, played piano in saloons around the Midwest and struggled to sell sheet music of his compositions. His success was modest until 1899, when he published "Maple Leaf Rag," named after a gentleman's club in Sedalia, Missouri. The tune took the country by storm, selling more than a million copies of sheet music, and created a national fad for ragtime.

From the beginning, ragtime and dance were closely joined. Writer James Weldon Johnson noted that ragtime "was music that demanded physical response, patting of the feet, drumming of the fingers, nodding of the head in time with the beat."[15] The biggest ragtime dance fad was the cakewalk, originally created by slaves as a high-stepping parody of whites.

At the height of the ragtime craze, the cakewalk was so prevalent that dozens of regional dance contests were held, leading to a national Cakewalk Jubilee and rivaling the music in popularity. Southern notes, "By the end of the century, the entertainment industry was sponsoring contests that offered two sets of prizes, one set for cakewalkers and the other set for ragtime pianists."[16]

Scott Joplin composed "Maple Leaf Rag" in 1899. The song was a best seller.

23

Sister Rosetta Tharpe, a successful gospel singer, performs in concert in 1944.

The Blues

As ragtime developed, a strikingly different style was taking shape. Ragtime was sophisticated, light, and refined; the blues was rough, dark, and emotionally charged. Ragtime was instrumental; the blues was vocal with instrumental accompaniment.

Ragtime was associated with affluence and the good life; the blues, frankly expressing a range of earthy emotions, was sung and most appreciated by poorer people. Nonetheless, many experts consider the blues to be the essential wellspring of all future popular American music, black or white. According to James Weldon Johnson, "It is from the blues that all that may be called American music derives its most distinctive characteristics."[17]

These characteristics were built on a simple but sturdy framework, one that provided ample room for variation. Each verse of a typical song had twelve bars—that is, twelve measures—in 4/4 time. Chord changes were a simple progression that rarely varied. Lyrics, meanwhile, were catchy and repetitive—typically two repeated lines followed by a rhyming third line.

The blues could be played on a piano, but most early blues musicians used whatever cheap, easily obtained, easily carried instruments they could find: guitars, harmonicas, jugs to blow into, or basses made from washtubs and broomsticks. They devised ways to make these simple instruments sound fresh, such as sliding the neck of a bottle over metal guitar strings for an eerie, mournful sound.

Blues and Gospel

Blues singing was highly emotional, by turns terrifying, seductive, heartbreaking, or hilarious. Vocalists improvised freely on basic song structures, borrowing the expressive bent notes, slurs, and shouts of the spirituals. This emphasized the close connection between the blues and religious music.

Black religious music was also developing rapidly, and by the early decades of the twentieth century, known as gospel, it was a highly stylized genre in its own right. Gospel was not strictly popular music, because it was meant for worship and not general consumption. However, gospel was popular music in the sense that many people listened to and loved it. Furthermore, it deeply influenced other forms of popular music.

Gospel, which counted among its greatest stars such singers as Mahalia Jackson and Sister Rosetta Tharpe, was characterized by passionate vocals, large choirs, and such instrumentation as a piano-organ combination. Its distinctive sound was an especially profound influence on the blues. As blues guitarist Johnny Shines once remarked: "Church music and the blues is all one and the same. They come out of the same soul, same heart, same body."[18]

"Ain't No First Blues!"

The exact birth date of the blues is unknown. An anonymous fiddler from New Orleans once commented: "The blues? Ain't no first blues! The blues always been."[19] Despite this uncertainty, however, scholars generally agree that the blues was flowering by the 1920s.

The music's precise birthplace is also unknown, although it was undoubtedly in the South. Several regions developed distinctive blues styles, notably Louisiana, East Texas, and the Piedmont area of North Carolina, but the Mississippi Delta is generally considered the cradle of the blues. This region of fertile cotton fields encompasses both sides of the Mississippi River and stretches roughly from Memphis south to Natchez, Mississippi.

At the time, the Mississippi Delta was home to the nation's densest population of African Americans. This community produced dozens of performers who shaped the blues in its early decades. Many were obscure even then, playing only for drinks or meals in local roadhouses, but others gained greater fame.

Early Blues Artists

Among the many classic blues artists of this early period were pianists Albert Ammons, Pete Johnson, and Meade Lux Lewis, all of whom pioneered a rollicking style called boogie-woogie. Others were guitarist-singers Charley Patton, Son House, Blind Lemon Jefferson, and Skip James, and singers Mamie Smith, Ma Rainey, and Bessie Smith (no relation to Mamie). But the archetypal blues artist was Robert Johnson.

Johnson's haunting vocals and virtuoso guitar playing set a high standard, and his story formed the template for the stereotypical bluesman's life of hard drinking and fast living. According to legend, Johnson sealed a pact with the devil at a crossroads in Clarksdale, Mississippi; in return for his soul, he could play and sing better than anyone else. But glory was short-lived; Johnson, still in his twenties, was fatally poisoned in 1938, probably by a girlfriend or a girlfriend's husband.

Another crucial figure during this period was Memphis composer and bandleader W.C. Handy. Handy called himself the Father of the Blues, but he was less an inventor than a popularizer. According to legend, he heard a man singing the blues in a train station and was inspired to transcribe it as written music—apparently becoming the first to do so. His compositions, including the wildly popular "Memphis Blues" and "St. Louis Blues," smoothed the music's rough edges, making it more appealing to a wide audience.

Blues trumpeter, band leader, and songwriter W.C. Handy (second from right) plays the trumpet with the Dixieland Octet in 1945.

A Rich Musical Gumbo

As the blues took shape, another fundamental genre of black music was gestating. The exact history of jazz is uncertain, but it is generally accepted that the music was born in New Orleans, came north to Chicago by way of traveling musicians, then spread to New York City—and from there around the world.

New Orleans was an appropriate birthplace. The Big Easy has always been the United States' most intensely musical town—a rich gumbo of French, Spanish, British, African American, and Caribbean influences. Around the turn of the twentieth century, New Orleans was a freewheeling port town. Ragtime pianists flocked there for work in the brothels, clubs, and saloons of Storyville, the city's official, tolerated red-light district.

New Orleans also had dozens of brass bands, usually associated with social and benevolent societies. Performing at such functions as picnics, parades, and funerals, these bands gave European marching music an African American lilt. Morgan and Barlow note, "They played popular martial [military] music, traditional spirituals, and minstrel favorites, all with a ragtime flavor."[20]

Down in New Orleans

Furthermore, the city featured many dance bands. Some were casual trios or quartets that played in halls with names like Funky Butt. Others were larger orchestras that played more formal, ballroom-style music for refined dances.

The Memphis Students and James Reese Europe

At the turn of the twentieth century, audiences began seeing the first large-scale black bands not based on minstrelsy tradition. These were influenced instead by more authentic African American genres and European concert- and dance-music styles. They combined traditional black instruments, such as the banjo, with traditional European concert-band instruments like saxophones and brass.

One prominent group was the Memphis Students, formed in 1905 by vaudevillian Ernest Hogan and Will Marion Cook, a violinist and classical composer. Based in New York City (despite its name), the Memphis Students was a very successful dance orchestra, backing vocal soloists with a full orchestra of banjos, mandolins, guitars, saxes, drums, violin, brass, and a double bass.

A member of the Memphis Students, James Reese Europe, went on to found many orchestral groups and form a fruitful partnership with a famous pair of white dancers, Irene and Vernon Castle. During World War I, Europe led a famous Army band—the 369th Infantry Division Band, nicknamed the Hell Fighters—that created a sensation when it toured the continent of Europe. The bandleader was on the verge of widespread fame when he was murdered in 1919, apparently by a disgruntled former band member.

New Orleans' musicians played wherever they could, becoming fluent in all of these styles, and absorbed everything; out of this musical stew came the classic Dixieland jazz sound. It incorporated ragged time, African-based rhythms, improvisation, and what Jelly Roll Morton called "the Spanish tinge"—slinky Latin rhythms imported from Cuba. A typical band was composed of a front line, usually a clarinet, trombone, and cornet or trumpet, supported by a rhythm section consisting of a guitar or banjo, piano, bass or tuba, and drums.

Unlike ragtime, which was entirely notated, jazz (or "jass," as it was called early on) emphasized improvisation. This ability to improvise was crucial, and jazz musicians looked down on those who could not. Playing with the heart was, to them, a far superior talent to being simply able to read music from a sheet.

Satchmo

Several stand out among New Orleans' jazz pioneers. One was Charles "Buddy" Bolden, a brilliant cornet player with a famously loud, clear tone; according to legend, people regularly heard him from 10 miles (16.09km) away and came running. Other outstanding New Orleans performers included Jelly Roll Morton, cornet player Joe "King" Oliver, trombonist Edward "Kid" Ory, and clarinet and soprano sax master Sidney Bechet.

But the greatest of them all was trumpet and cornet player (and sometimes singer) Louis Armstrong. Armstrong was a singular genius, a bighearted individual, and, arguably, the most important figure in jazz history. Many aficionados consider him one of the greatest American musicians in any genre, ever.

Satchmo, as he was fondly known, burst onto the national scene in the 1920s with Kid Ory's Creole Jazz Band. Armstrong's first solo recordings, the *Hot Five/Hot Seven* discs, set unparalleled standards for imagination, technique, and sheer joy in playing. His overall influence is incalculable; as another genius of jazz, Miles Davis, once remarked, "You can't play anything on a horn that Louis hasn't played."[21]

Musical Theater

Jazz eventually absorbed ragtime as a style. Meanwhile, the minstrel show and its crude stereotypes were also dying, replaced by

Louis Armstrong, considered by many to be the greatest of jazz trumpeters, warms up for a concert.

musical theater. This genre was not exclusively by or for African Americans, and it began well before the 1920s, but black musical theater flowered during those years.

One especially influential show was 1921's *Shuffle Along*, the first hit musical produced, created, and performed entirely by African Americans. It was so popular during its Broadway run that the New York City traffic department made the street in front of the theater one-way to better accommodate crowds.

Shuffle Along introduced a number of hit songs, including "I'm Just Wild About Harry." It launched three future stars: Florence Mills, Paul Robeson, and Josephine Baker. And it broke new ground by depicting dignified, sophisticated, and intelligent characters—a far cry from the minstrel era.

Other outstanding shows included *Running Wild*, which launched a dance sensation called the Charleston. *Blackbirds of 1928* introduced Bill "Bojangles" Robinson, soon to become the king of tap dancers. And *Hot Chocolates* featured the ebullient pianist-singer-comedian Thomas "Fats" Waller performing some of his most famous compositions, including "Ain't Misbehavin'."

Smiling His Way into People's Hearts

Also on the rise was vaudeville, variety programs presenting everything from comedy and singing to animal acts and dancers. Thanks to newly built rail lines across the country, circuits for vaudeville shows became so widespread that even the smallest town could see new acts every week. Jasen and Jones note, "Vaudeville blanketed America as the . . . minstrel shows never had, reaching into towns large and small, and the czars of the circuits sent their talent everywhere."[22]

For black vaudevillians, the main circuit was the Theater Owners Booking Association (TOBA), a string of theaters

Preparing to Flee

The musical *Shuffle Along*, which premiered in 1921, broke a number of important racial barriers. One was that, until then, a romantic love scene between African Americans had never been shown onstage. The accepted belief was such a scene had to be played for broad comedy, since white audiences would be uncomfortable with a serious one.

Shuffle Along changed all that. At the premiere of the show, during a love scene between black characters, composer Eubie Blake was onstage playing piano for the romantic ballad "Love Will Find a Way." But lyricist Noble Sissle and others involved in the show's production were at the stage door, ready to flee if the theater audience threatened to erupt in violence. To their relief, the scene was met with great applause. Another wall in the racial divide had come tumbling down.

throughout the South, Midwest, and East. At its peak, TOBA had more than fifty theaters and hundreds of performers. Life on TOBA was rough and the pay was poor; among performers, the initials stood for "Tough on Black Asses." Still, it provided a reasonable living for many.

Occasionally, vaudeville performers moved on to real stardom, such as the husband-and-wife comedians known as Butterbeans and Susie. Another was comic Bert Williams, of whom the African American leader Booker T. Washington remarked: "He has done more for our race than I have. He has smiled his way into people's hearts; I have been obliged to fight my way."[23]

Mamie Smith, pictured here with the Jazz Hounds, was the most popular vocalist of the 1920s.

Early Recordings

Williams was one of the many performers of the era who benefited from a new invention: the phonograph record. Since the earliest days of the technology, when recordings were made on fragile glass or wax cylinders, ragtime, blues, spirituals, and jazz had been occasionally recorded. However, recordings of black popular music remained rare for some years, since record company owners doubted they would sell.

A black entrepreneur, Perry Bradford, proved them wrong in 1920. Bradford convinced the Okeh record company to record Mamie Smith singing "Crazy Blues." It was a runaway success, Smith became one of the decade's most popular vocalists, and the way was paved for others.

The success of "Crazy Blues" inspired several companies to create divisions just for race records, a term for any black-oriented recording. By 1925, hundreds of race titles were appearing every year, and African Americans were buying 6 million discs annually just from the top three companies featuring them.

Most of the performers on these records received only a tiny fraction of the money they earned. Writer Arthur Kempton asserts, for example, that "Bessie Smith made a million dollars for Columbia Records in ten years. For this she was paid $28,575."[24] Nonetheless, the advent of records considerably brightened the future for black performers.

The Great Depression

The good times did not last long. The onset in 1929 of a devastating economic crash, the Great Depression, created chaos. People were starving and had precious little money to spare for records, nightclubs, or theaters. Within a few years, the music industry collapsed almost completely.

A number of vaudeville circuits, including TOBA, went out of business. In the record industry, annual sales overall fell from $100 million in 1927 to $6 million in 1933. A typical race record sold about ten thousand copies in the mid-1920s; by 1932, that average plummeted to four hundred.

Several positive factors offset this grim picture. Prohibition, the national ban on liquor from 1920 to 1933, was a huge boon for musicians because of the spectacular rise in the number of speakeasies—illegal nightclubs—needing live entertainment. The rising popularity of the jukebox also helped boost record sales. Also, black musicians slowly began making inroads on radio, another recent invention that was quickly blanketing the nation.

Overall, by the mid-1930s, black popular music was entering mainstream American culture. The worst stereotypes were disappearing; African American musicians and songwriters were being recognized as innovative, financially successful style setters. It was time for the next major development.

Chapter Three

From Swing to Bebop

As black pop music moved into the 1930s and early 1940s, several genres continued to evolve. The most widespread was jazz. In particular, a style of jazz called swing dominated musical tastes so thoroughly that the era is known as the Swing Years.

Swing, also called big band music, was popular for several reasons. It was good for dancing. Its featured vocalists were attractive. And its catchy melodies and rhythms were fun to listen to. Thanks to swing's accessibility, audiences during the Swing Years were the largest that jazz ever had.

The Big Band Theory

Two key figures in swing were Fletcher Henderson, a pianist and bandleader, and his gifted arranger, Don Redman. (An arranger dictates when and how the various parts of a band or orchestra play.) Henderson's orchestra, based in New York City, embodied the ways in which swing differed from its older cousin, New Orleans jazz.

One difference was size. In contrast to a typical New Orleans–style group of five or six, a band like Henderson's had ten, twelve, or more players, grouped into three sections:

rhythm (piano, guitar, bass, drums), brass (trumpets and trombones), and reeds (saxophones and clarinets). The bandleader was typically the conductor and often played an instrument as well.

This expanded size dictated a change in style. Large groups could not improvise simultaneously, as Dixieland bands did, without creating chaos. Swing thus had improvisation by soloists with simplified group backing, which alternated with written-out sections where the orchestra played as a single unit.

Another characteristic of swing was the contrast between brass and reed sections, which built excitement by creating call-and-response "battles." Swing also featured singers more prominently than earlier styles. And swing created a new rhythmic standard as well: steady accents on all four beats, a flowing rhythm that replaced the two-beat rhythm of Dixieland.

Fletcher Henderson (seated at the piano, far right) and his band, pictured here in 1924, pioneered the swing sound.

Club patrons in Harlem dance the jitterbug in the mid-1930s.

Top Bands

The new style took hold just as the Depression was deepening. Dancing to a swing band was a cheap pastime, one that even the poor could afford. Hundreds of orchestras and ballrooms sprang up across the country to accommodate dancers looking for an affordable night out.

White musicians were quick to jump on the fad. Some white bandleaders, including Paul Whiteman, played watered-down, semiorchestral swing, although Whiteman was considered too corny for purists. Others, like Glenn Miller, Artie Shaw, and Benny Goodman, led inventive and genuinely swinging bands. Goodman was also a pioneer with racially integrated groups at a time when this was still controversial.

Competition was fierce for white and black bands alike, and top ensembles commanded top dollar. Among the big-league

African American bandleaders, besides Henderson, were Jimmie Lunceford, Earl "Fatha" Hines, Luis Russell, Chick Webb, and Cab Calloway. At the top, however, were two pianist-bandleaders with royal nicknames: Edward Ellington and William Basie, better known as the Duke and the Count.

The Duke

In New York City, the debonair Duke Ellington ruled. Ellington's crucial role in the history of jazz cannot be overstated; to many, he is second in importance only to Louis Armstrong. Writer Albert Murray notes, "I don't think anybody has achieved a higher synthesis of the American experience than Duke Ellington expressed in his music."[25]

Ellington stood out because of his brilliantly imaginative, highly sophisticated compositions and the outstanding individuals in his orchestra. Swing music often seemed interchangeable, playable by any competent group, but Ellington compositions were always custom crafted for certain players.

It was thus impossible to separate individual players from the Ellington sound. His piece "Warm Hills," for instance, needed the liquid, sensuous tone of alto saxophonist Johnny Hodges to sound right. Jazz critic Whitney Balliett comments: "Most of the big bands . . . came in two distinct parts—their leaders . . . and the disposable hired help. But Ellington and his musicians were indivisible."[26]

The Count

The other giant of swing, Count Basie, made his reputation in Kansas City, Missouri. During the swing era, K.C., as Kansas City was known, was a rail center where vice was openly tolerated, and the musicians who frequented the city's many clubs and cabarets developed their own distinctive swing.

The K.C. sound, sometimes called jump blues, was a robust genre built around simple, repeated figures called riffs. Its chief soloists were trumpeters and tenor saxophonists who were deeply influenced by the blues. Indeed, the blues was its cornerstone, historian Southern notes: "Blues could . . . fit any mood; played fast, it generated excitement, and played slowly, it could be as melancholy as desired."[27]

Harlem Nightclubs

In 1927, Duke Ellington began the engagement that brought him to fame. This was an extended stay at the Cotton Club in Harlem, the black neighborhood of Manhattan that was the center of African American cultural life. Harlem had the best nightclubs in the world, both during and after Prohibition, and the best of the best was the elegant Cotton Club, with its red-tuxedoed waiters and lavish, if bizarre, decor: log cabin outside, jungle inside, Southern plantation on the bandstand.

The customers at the Cotton Club were almost completely white, though blacks were allowed in if they were celebrities. All the entertainers, however, were African American. They took part in elaborate floor shows featuring singers, dancers, comedians, and chorus girls in showy costumes that changed with every number.

The Cotton Club in Harlem was a popular venue for singers, dancers, and musicians.

Count Basie made a name for himself in Kansas City, Missouri, during the swing era.

Kansas City bands were collectively known as territory bands, because they played a regular circuit of clubs around the Midwest. Among the top territory bands were those fronted by pianists Jay McShann and Mary Lou Williams. But Basie was the king.

His juggernaut band was anchored by a rock-solid rhythm section featuring the leader's lean, elegant piano. Other featured soloists included saxophonists Lester Young and Hershel Evans and trumpeter Buck Clayton. Basie's singers included, at various times, such gifted performers as Joe Williams, Big Joe Turner, Helen Humes, and Jimmy Rushing—a man so portly he was nicknamed Mister Five by Five.

Soloists and Vocalists

The Ellington and Basie bands, big ensembles working together, personified the way in which swing was primarily a group effort.

But a number of gifted soloists also emerged during these years. For example, the many outstanding pianists, in addition to Ellington and Basie, included Earl "Fatha" Hines, Teddy Wilson, and Art Tatum.

The tenor sax was not a common jazz instrument until the swing years, when soloists like Coleman Hawkins and Ben Webster made it a frontline instrument. Trumpet standouts included Harry "Sweets" Edison, Roy Eldridge, and Buck Clayton.

Vocalists were also important to big bands. Typically, singers performed part of a song before stepping aside for other soloists, though often featured spots gave them greater prominence. Some singers were sweet and refined; others were fire-breathing shouters. In any case, virtually every swing band had at least one good vocalist on hand. An exception was the Ellington orchestra,

Coleman Hawkins, playing the saxophone, performs on stage with his band in 1950.

which prevailed mostly on the strength of its brilliant leader and his instrumentalists.

Three Queens of Song

Three female singers in particular stood out during the swing years. The spectacularly gifted Ella Fitzgerald won a talent contest as a teenager, joined Chick Webb's band, led it after Webb's death, and went on to a long solo career. Fitzgerald was renowned for her ability to scat, or create long, wordless strings of instrumental-like improvisations.

Equally talented was the honey-voiced Sarah Vaughan. Like Fitzgerald, Vaughan was blessed with flawless pitch, beautiful tone, and a range of operatic size and quality. Also like Fitzgerald, she had a long career that stretched far beyond the swing years.

A third female singer of the era, Billie Holiday, differed sharply from Fitzgerald and Vaughan in style. Holiday had a limited range and rarely strayed far from the melody. But she also had brilliant, exquisite timing and an unforgettably bittersweet voice. It mirrored the difficulties and sadness the singer experienced in her life, projecting to her audiences a deep sense of loneliness and yearning.

"We Called Ourselves Modern"

Swing lasted through World War II (1941–1945), but, as with all musical genres, it was eventually replaced by a new style. When swing fell from favor, big bands could not survive; virtually every leader had to trim to a five- or six-person combo. An exception was Ellington, who managed to keep his large group intact.

In swing's place came bebop, or simply bop. The name was a playful take on the music's staccato rhythms, although in its early days it had no name. Drummer Kenny Clarke recalls: "The music wasn't called bop [at first]. In fact, we had no name for the music. We called ourselves modern."[28]

Bebop was a radical departure. It was not just music; it was part of a lifestyle, a self-contained subculture that required new ways of talking (in hipster jive), acting (always cool), and dressing (in berets, floppy bow ties, and flamboyant suits). Bop was intellectual, urbanized, and extremely hip. Drugs, long part of the jazz scene, now became even more closely connected with it; heroin, in particular, claimed many victims among the boppers.

Exquisite Poetry out of Nothing

◼

Billie Holiday stood out among jazz singers of the era not because of the range of her voice or her ability to improvise, but because her vocal instrument carried an extraordinary emotional punch. Music critic John Chilton notes:

> The timbre of her voice was completely individual, and her incredible sense of rhythm and intuitive knowledge of harmony enabled her to phrase songs in a unique way. She could reshape the bleakest melody into something that offered a vast range of emotions to her listeners; her artistry and timing gave her the ability to make poetry out of the most banal lyrics.

Quoted in Jennifer Blue, "Finding the Rhythm of Blues in Children's Poetry, Art, and Music," Yale-New Haven Teachers Institute. www.yale.edu/ynhti/curriculum/units/1997/5/97.05.04.x.html.

Bop Develops

The new music primarily developed in New York City clubs like Minton's. Minton's frequently hosted after-hours jam sessions when virtuoso musicians tried to outdo each other. Its house band included, besides Clarke, trumpeter Dizzy Gillespie, pianist Thelonious Monk, guitarist Charlie Christian, and alto saxophonist Charlie Parker. Many others emerged as bop pioneers as well, among them saxophonists Dexter Gordon, John Coltrane, and Sonny Rollins; trumpeter Miles Davis; drummer Max Roach; bassist Charlie Mingus; and pianist Bud Powell.

Bop bands were usually small groups: rhythm sections consisting of piano, bass, and drums backing one to three saxophones and/or brass instruments. Occasionally, other instruments, such as guitars or vibraphones, were used as well. Vocals were downplayed, though bebop did have such outstanding singers as Eddie Jefferson, King Pleasure, and the ethereal Betty Carter.

The music's foundations were a bold departure from swing. Its brash style emphasized complex rhythms, dissonant harmonies, and unusual keys and tempos. Often its tunes were original, but

Kenny Clarke, a pioneer of the bop style, plays drums during a recording session in 1954.

frequently, existing songs were reworked until they were virtually unrecognizable. For example, Charlie Parker's "Anthropology" used the basic structure of an earlier song, George Gershwin's "I Got Rhythm."

Bop was was a hard, aggressive, urbanized sound. It was in tune with an accelerated and increasingly industrialized postwar world. Trumpeter Gillespie recalls that bop was "fast and furious, . . . going this way and that way; it might've looked and sounded like bedlam, but it really wasn't."[29]

Varieties of Bop

Bop took itself quite seriously. What beboppers played was, to them, not simple dance music but serious art that required serious listening. Miles Davis personified this by deliberately turning his back onstage, overtly distancing himself from his audience.

Needless to say, not everyone liked the new style. For fans of older jazz, bop seemed cold and difficult to follow, offering nothing beyond showy style. One New York newspaper critic sniffed that boppers were nothing more than "a cult of beret-topped, chin-whiskered followers with flashy clothes and big, flowing bow ties."[30]

Nonetheless, bop was on the cutting edge of jazz well into the 1950s and spawned many subgroups—hard bop, West Coast, cool, and more. Each had its own distinctive elements; for example, cool bop's sound was, as the name implies, detached and dispassionate. It was typified by Miles Davis's minimalist solos, in which the silence between notes was as eloquent as the notes themselves.

Electric Blues

Despite this proliferation of styles, bebop's defiant attitude condemned it to remain a cult genre. It lost the wide audience that swing once enjoyed, and jazz was no longer music for light entertainment and dancing. That role was filled, at least in part, by the blues—which itself was undergoing changes.

Until the mid-1940s, the blues had been acoustic folk music from the rural South. That style did not die out, but a new form developed during the late 1940s and 1950s: electric blues, also called urban blues. As the name suggests, this style used a still-new technology—amplification—to change its sound radically.

This change mirrored social changes among African Americans. Throughout the 1930s and 1940s, millions of black

No Titles

———————◼———————

Trumpeter Dizzy Gillespie, in this passage, talks about the origins of the word *bebop*: "We played a lot of original tunes that didn't have titles. We just wrote an introduction and first chorus. I'd say, 'Dee-da-pa-da-n-de-bop . . .' and we'd go into it. People, when they'd wanna ask for one of those numbers and didn't know the name, would ask for bebop. And the press picked it up and started calling it bebop."

Dizzy Gillespie and Al Fraser, *To Be or Not to Bop*. New York: Doubleday, 1979, p. 207.

Singer, songwriter, and guitarist Muddy Waters was the most famous of the Chicago bluesmen.

southerners had continued to migrate to industrialized cities in the North, Midwest, and West. Among them were a number of talented blues musicians.

These performers found that their music was easier to hear in crowded dance halls if they used full drum kits and electric bass guitars. Furthermore, amplifying instruments like guitars and harmonicas gave the musicians a wide range of new sounds. Formerly a languid and quiet style, the blues when amplified took on a driving, aggressive edge—one that appealed strongly to dance-hall fans.

Chicago Blues

Regional blues styles developed in cities like Memphis, which boasted such players as guitarist B.B. King, and Los Angeles, which counted another guitarist, Aaron "T-Bone" Walker, among its stars. But the center for electric blues was Chicago. The city's South Side, in particular, was the place for this exciting new music.

Pianist Otis Spann, harmonica player-singer Howlin' Wolf (Chester Burnett), and bassist-composer Willie Dixon were just three of Chicago's most prominent blues musicians. Singer Koko Taylor, harmonica virtuoso James Cotton, and guitarist-singer Otis Rush were three more. But the undisputed king of Chicago blues was McKinley Morganfield, better known as Muddy Waters, a singer, guitarist, and songwriter whose powerhouse bands always included the cream of Chicago's bluesmen.

A former tractor driver from Mississippi, Waters embodied the connection between the older, acoustic Delta blues and the exciting new style he helped create. His songs, including "I'm a Man" and "Mannish Boy," balance the laid-back ease of country blues with the gritty intensity of the electric version. Music scholar Pete Welding writes, "From the start it was [Waters] who dominated the music, who led the way."[31]

Records

Blues musicians—and other black recording artists, for that matter—benefited during this period from continuing advances in recording technology. This was a welcome change from the lean war years. During that period, record sales had been low, in part due to a shortage of the shellac used to manufacture them (it was needed for the defense industry).

In the postwar years, with shellac again available, record sales rose. In addition, several technological breakthroughs had recently been made. One was magnetic tape, which made the tape recorder possible. Another was the long-playing (LP) record, which made it possible to record up to twenty five minutes on a side, a huge improvement over the old limit of about three minutes.

Although the sales of singles remained strong, artists were eager to exploit the possibilities offered by the LP. For example, Miles Davis and an ingenious arranger, Gil Evans, recorded a series of extended suites, including the now-classic "Sketches of Spain." Recording these would have been impossible without the extended LP format.

Advancing

In part because of the LP's capabilities, record sales boomed in the 1950s for many African Americans. A prime example was Nat "King" Cole, who started his career as a bebop piano player but found lasting fame as a singer. As a pianist, Cole had only moderate success, but his remarkable voice sold tens of millions of copies of such tunes as "The Christmas Song" and "Mona Lisa." This made Cole, far and away, the most successful black performer of his day and one of the most successful performers of any race or era.

Cole's success—and he was just one of many—indicated how far black popular music had come. Another sign was the rise of

Oscar Moore, Johnny Miller, and Nat King Cole (left to right) pose with their instruments in this 1945 photo. Cole had more success as a singer than as a pianist.

the annual summer jazz festival, including famous events at Newport, Rhode Island, and Monterey, California. Furthermore, jazz was by now being taught in universities, and the American government was asking artists like Louis Armstrong to serve as goodwill ambassadors overseas.

Black musicians had a long way to go before reaching anything like equality with their white counterparts, in record sales or any other measure. Nonetheless, enormous strides had been made since the beginning of the century. Music historians William Barlow and Cheryl Finley note, "The music born in the saloons and bordellos of New Orleans was now being performed on the stages of metropolitan concert halls throughout the world."[32]

But even greater changes were yet to come. The years after the war—the late 1940s and early 1950s—saw the birth of an emotional, hard-driving dance music called rhythm and blues.

Chapter Four

R&B and Rock and Roll

Rhythm and blues—R&B for short—was the dominant popular music style of the postwar years. Jerry Wexler, who wrote for *Billboard*, a music-industry magazine that compiles sales charts, popularized the term in 1947. The new genre was such a hit that by 1949 *Billboard* had a chart specifically for it, and "rhythm and blues" replaced the outdated "race music" to describe black pop music in general.

R&B was a hybrid of three basic elements: electric blues, gospel, and the honking, tenor-sax driven jazz of the Midwest territory bands. The result vividly reflected the full gamut of modern, urban black life. To writer Arnold Shaw, R&B "embodied the fervor of gospel music, the throbbing vigor of boogie woogie, the jump beat of swing, and the gutsiness and sexuality of life in the black ghetto."[33]

The typical R&B band was a small, tightly knit combo. Its rhythm section—electric guitar, piano, bass (usually electric), and drums—was based on that of a typical electric blues band. R&B bands also usually added a saxophone or saxophone-trumpet combination.

Virtually all R&B bands also had a vocalist, who often doubled on an instrument. Vocals, crucial in R&B, were strongly influenced by the unpolished style of gospel, conveying all the passion of a great preacher or gospel singer and using gospel techniques like melisma and falsetto (very high-pitched singing). The influence of religious music on R&B was so strong that Wexler later commented, "If I understood then what I know now, I would have called it rhythm and gospel."[34]

"Ain't Nobody Here but Us Chickens"

R&B developed in several cities, and the identity of the first true R&B artist is the source of ongoing debate. Texan Amos Milburn, Californians Saunders King and Roy Brown, and Nebraskan Wynonie Harris are only four of the many contenders. But an enormously energetic singer-saxophonist, Louis Jordan, perhaps best represented the style's early years, bridging the period between the decline of swing and the full flowering of R&B.

Jordan, born in Arkansas, was based in New York. He and his band, the Tympany Five, played a wide variety of material, from

Louis Jordan (center) and his band, Tympany Five, played a variety of music styles including blues, jazz, and pop.

Covering Up the Blues

————————————■————————————

R&B pioneer Ruth Brown comments on the feelings behind the music she sang:

> We were working under all kinds of adverse situations. . . . Consequently, there was a lot of hurt that went along with it. What really sustained us was the music. All of the things that went wrong during the travels, or the harassment, you took that out onstage. You got up and started to sing, and I think that's where the feeling for the lyric comes from. It was a total experience. The rhythm covered up for the blues. That's my estimation of what rhythm and blues was. The rhythm, the beat, covered up the blues, but the blues was inside.

Quoted in Ted Fox, *Showtime at the Apollo.* New York: Da Capo, 1993, p. 170.

straightforward blues to commercial pop songs and territory-style jump jazz. Jordan is best remembered, however, for witty novelty tunes like "Is You Is or Is You Ain't My Baby?" and "Ain't Nobody Here but Us Chickens."

Jordan's good-time manner and eclectic material proved wildly popular. His records sold in the millions, and his style was copied by combos everywhere. Music professor Guthrie P. Ramsey Jr. writes: "Jordan's postwar rhythm and blues cast a long shadow of influence. It set the stage for a watershed . . . movement that would dominate popular music in the following decades."[35]

Beyond Jordan's influence, distinctive R&B was stirring in a number of places. New Orleans, for example, continued to produce outstanding performers, such as the eccentric singer-pianist Professor Longhair. The Professor's virtuoso playing was heavily laced with Cuban rumba rhythms and other exotic influences. He enjoyed giving his bands colorful names, such as Professor Longhair and His Shuffling Hungarians.

The Kings of Rhythm released one of rock and roll's earliest songs, "Rocket 88."

Many cities besides New Orleans, including New York, Chicago, Memphis, and Los Angeles, also bred distinctive styles and performers. Los Angeles, for example, was home to many from the South and Southwest who had moved there in search of defense-industry jobs. They liked territory-style jump blues and favored such performers as guitarist T-Bone Walker.

Radio and Records

Radio helped popularize R&B in its earliest days. Several idiosyncratic disc jockeys (DJs), including Poppa Stoppa in New Orleans and Dewey Phillips in Memphis, featured it on their shows. While many pioneering R&B DJs were white, a few were black; prominent among these were Rufus Thomas and B.B. King—both based in Memphis, and both noted stage performers as well.

Dozens of independent record labels also helped spread the music. They were able to sign up R&B bands because larger record companies mostly ignored the genre. R&B was thus almost exclusively the province of scrappy little companies like Specialty (Los Angeles), Sun (Memphis), Atlantic (New York City), Ace (New Orleans), Savoy (Newark), Peacock (Houston), and Chess (Chicago).

But these small companies were strictly regional and limited in their ability to distribute records. Only a handful of R&B artists, like Jordan, had national reputations. Most were local stars, scuffling for work on regional dance circuits and making the occasional record. Guitarist Ike Turner, for instance, was a star around Memphis, but few people outside the region knew him. R&B as a whole did not take off until it evolved into something new: rock and roll.

R&B Becomes R&R

The exact point of rock and roll's birth is shrouded in mystery and remains the source of spirited discussion among music historians. They generally agree, however, that the shift was generational; rock and roll was music specifically for teenagers. Its air of rebellion strongly appealed to the younger generation, and since teenagers had increasing amounts of money to spend in the postwar years, the music became big business.

In the late 1940s and early 1950s, several singers made recordings that were strong contenders for the title of first rock-and-roll record. Among these were Roy Brown's "Good Rockin'

Making Do

The song that many consider the first true rock-and-roll tune, Ike Turner's "Rocket 88," features a distinctive fuzzed-out sound from the band's lead guitarist. The story behind how that sound came to be illustrates the casual nature of pop record production in the early 1950s.

Lead guitarist Willie Kizart's amp had fallen from his car on the way to the studio, and the speaker cone burst. But the band and producer Sam Phillips, later a legendary figure through his work with Elvis Presley, were too impatient to get it fixed. Phillips recalls, "It would probably have taken a couple of days [to fix it], so we started playing around with the damn thing. I stuffed a little paper in there where the speaker cone was ruptured, and it sounded good."

Quoted in Robert Palmer, *Rock and Roll: An Unruly History.* New York: Harmony, 1995, p. 202.

Tonight," Amos Milburn's "Chicken Shack Boogie," and Little Willie Littlefield's "K.C. Loving" (later rewritten as "Kansas City").

Another likely candidate was "Rocket 88." This robust tune was recorded in Memphis in 1951 by Ike Turner's band, the Kings of Rhythm. With its grainy vocals, fuzzy guitar, and timeless subject matter (a car), "Rocket 88" clearly indicated rock and roll's musical direction and interests.

As had happened so often before, white performers quickly picked up a black trend. Their versions, usually tamer, appealed to wider audiences and thus were far more successful financially. Rock and roll's first national hit—"Crazy Man Crazy" in 1953—was thus by a white musician, Bill Haley.

"Brown Eyed Handsome Man"

A tidal wave of performers—the first generation of rockers, white and black alike—followed Haley's success. Between 1953 and 1958, early rock's glory years, hundreds of potential stars fought for prominence. One—a teenager named Elvis Presley—would soon be the biggest of them all, at least financially. Among the others, three in particular stood out.

The first, Chuck Berry, is considered by many to be rock's true father. As an aspiring bandleader in St. Louis, Berry achieved stardom with a style deeply influenced by midwestern jump blues, characterized by driving, elastic guitar riffs and charismatic performances that included his trademark duck walk.

But Berry's special genius lay in his songwriting. Among the prolific composer's many tunes were "Maybellene," "Sweet Little Sixteen," "Johnny B. Goode," "Brown Eyed Handsome Man," "The Promised Land," and "Roll Over Beethoven." Each was a model of verbal economy and wit, and they resonated deeply with the teenagers of the day. Berry's songs still inspire; according to writer Ben Fong-Torres, they are "a body of highly American imagery from which rock & roll continues to feed."[36]

The Fat Man

Another outstanding early rocker was a product of New Orleans: Antoine "Fats" Domino. Of all the performers bred in the Big Easy during this period, none rose higher than Domino. He was already a seasoned pro when rock and roll went national in the early 1950s; he had scored his first regional R&B hit ("The Fat Man") back in 1949, and he had been routinely producing hit after hit ever since.

Like many performers, Domino cheerfully blurred the line between R&B and rock and roll, seeming to care little for distinctions. No matter what his music was called, Domino kept turning out hits. "Ain't That a Shame," "Blue Monday," "Blueberry Hill," and "Walkin' to New Orleans" were just four of the twenty-three gold records—singles that sold a million or more copies—that he racked up during his peak years.

Domino's amiable personality, sharply at odds with the surly attitude typical of early rockers, was part of his appeal. The music was just as temperate, blending a rolling piano with Domino's genial

Fats Domino combined the sounds of R&B and rock and roll in his songs.

voice. It was a unique combination, New Orleans studio owner Cosimo Matassa comments: "He could be singing the national anthem, you'd still know by the time he said two words it was him, obviously, unmistakably, and pleasurably him."[37]

The Georgia Peach

A third giant of the era hailed from Macon, Georgia: piano-thumping Richard Penniman, better known as Little Richard. The Georgia Peach may not have been the most gifted of the early rockers, but he was one of the wildest. No one had more attitude than Little Richard.

Little Richard wails out a tune during a 1956 concert in Toronto, Canada.

Richard's stage persona was built around his outrageous looks: towering hairdo, heavy makeup, flamboyant wardrobe, and ambiguous sexuality. Musically, Richard's sound paired his pliant, gospel-drenched voice with his band's rugged musicianship. And then there were his teasing nonsense lyrics, of which "A-womp-bomp-a-loo-bop-a-womp-bam-boom!" is typical.

Richard's biggest hits included "Tutti Frutti," "Long Tall Sally," and "Good Golly Miss Molly," and they made him hugely successful. But Richard, the product of a devoutly religious upbringing, was constantly torn between his deep faith and the temptations of a performer's lifestyle. At the peak of his career, the singer abandoned music for Bible study, though afterward he periodically returned to the rock-and-roll life.

Doo-Wop

While Little Richard and others perfected rock and roll, others favored more traditional genres. One development was doo-wop, a style of unaccompanied vocal music. Doo-wop was born when teenagers in cities like New York and Philadelphia gathered on corners to sing. Instruments were rare, so they made music solely with their voices.

Doo-wop was a nonreligious version of the male quartet style, a major form of gospel singing. These quartets often had five or six members, despite the name. Typically, a gospel quartet sang repeated phrases or nonsense syllables, harmonizing behind a lead vocalist's improvisations. Contrast was created through occasional solos by a falsetto singer or a deep, rumbling bass voice.

Like some gospel quartets, doo-wop groups occasionally used instrumental backing, but the emphasis remained on a cappella (unaccompanied) vocals. Close-harmony group singing had already reached mainstream pop, in the form of smooth groups like the Ink Spots and the Mills Brothers. With doo-wop, it expanded into the less polished world of teen music.

Birds, Cars, and Romance

Classic doo-wop songs included "Goodnight, Sweetheart, Goodnight" by the Spaniels, "Earth Angel" by the Penguins, and "Crying in the Chapel" by the Orioles. Other prominent doo-woppers were named after birds (Ravens, Penguins, Robins, Flamingoes, Falcons), cars (Cadillacs, Lincolns, El Dorados, Impalas), and romantic images (Moonglows, Hearts, Charms, Heartbeats, Dream Lovers).

Several outstanding singers emerged from doo-wop as solo stars. One was sweet-voiced Clyde McPhatter, who first came to fame with Billy Ward and the Dominoes, then formed his own group, the Drifters, before going solo. Among McPhatter's many hits (with the Drifters or on his own) were "Money Honey" and a swaggering version of the old standby "White Christmas."

Another star was the soulful Ben E. King, who sang with the Drifters before going solo. King's many classics include "Save the Last Dance for Me," "Spanish Harlem," and "Stand by Me." A third major figure was Jackie Wilson, like McPhatter a former member of the Dominoes. Wilson's dramatic voice and electrifying stage presence immortalized such songs as "Higher and Higher" and "Lonely Teardrops."

Girl Groups

The female equivalents to doo-wop singers were girl groups. They were relatively rare in the mid-1950s, when doo-wop was strong, but girl groups began to dominate in the late 1950s. By the early 1960s, girl groups ruled.

Like their male counterparts, girl groups specialized in close harmonies. One big difference was that they did not sing a cappella, perhaps because the groups lacked deep bass voices to provide bottom for their sound. Instead, small combos or orchestras backed them.

Among the most prominent were the Chiffons, Popsicles, Chantels, Dixie Cups, Crystals, Ronettes, Toys, and Shangri-Las. One of the top groups was the Shirelles, whose magnificent 1960 recording of "Will You Love Me Tomorrow?" became the first number one song by a girl group.

"Will You Love Me Tomorrow?" was typical of the romantic love songs performed by girl groups; others included "He's So Fine" by the Chiffons and "Chapel of Love" by the Dixie Cups. But some were edgier. "The Leader of the Pack" by the Shangri-Las (a rare, white girl group) emphasized their bad-girl image with its tragic tale of the lead singer's true love, the doomed head of a motorcycle gang.

The Chiffons was one of many successful girl groups of the 1960s.

The Brill Building

Inevitably, doo-woppers and girl groups caught the attention of the commercial music industry. Teen music was becoming big business, and the big record companies were moving in. They needed huge volumes of teen music to sell, and this led to the creation of a large pool of professional songwriters, music publishers, and producers.

Hundreds of these professionals were headquartered in New York City's Brill Building. They developed a style so recognizable that music historians often refer to it as the Brill Building Sound. Some were mediocre, grinding out material to make a

Howling on Air

———■———

Part of the success of R&B and its younger sibling, rock and roll, was due to the rise of radio shows specializing in the music. A number of disc jockeys, both black and white, helped introduce the music to a mainstream audience.

Among them were Dewey Phillips in Memphis and the mysterious Bob "Wolfman Jack" Smith, whose gravelly voiced broadcasts came from a station just across the Mexican border. Such stations were called pirate stations because they were not subject to regulation by American authorities. One especially influential station was WLAC in Nashville. Thanks to the station's powerful 50,000-watt signal, its nighttime R&B show could be heard throughout much of the eastern half of the country.

But the most prominent rock-and-roll radio personality was a white disc jockey named Alan Freed. In 1951, Freed began hosting a Cleveland radio show, primarily for white audiences, called *Moondog's Rock 'n' Roll Party*. The term *rock 'n' roll* or its variants had been used in the black community for years, denoting both sex and a musical style, but Freed was the first to use it with mainstream audiences. Freed's frantic on-air manner fit the music he played. He howled like a wolf, beat his fist in time to the music in front of an open mike, talked in nonstop jive patter, and even drank alcohol openly while on air.

fast buck; others were remarkably talented. Unlike most of the singers who performed their material, the Brill Building's residents were primarily white.

Among those associated with the Brill Building were Jerry Leiber and Mike Stoller, who wrote and produced wry tunes like "Hound Dog," "Yakety Yak," and "Jailhouse Rock" for groups like the Coasters. Another prominent team was Mort Shuman and Doc Pomus; typical of their emotionally complex songs was "Save the Last Dance for Me" for the Drifters. Another Pomus-Shuman song, "Teenager in Love," was so popular that at one point three different versions appeared simultaneously on sales charts in England.

Still another memorable partnership was the husband-wife team of Gerry Goffin and Carole King. While some of their efforts were best forgotten ("Let's Turkey Trot"), they produced dozens of enduring hits, including "Up on the Roof," "Will You Love Me Tomorrow?" and "The Loco-Motion," which was recorded by the pair's babysitter, Little Eva.

"So Much Going On"

Teenaged singers associated with the Brill Building were by no means the only black pop performers during this period; older musicians were still going strong. Powerful R&B and blues singers like Ruth Brown, Lavern Baker, and Big Joe Turner remained enduringly popular. Smooth pop crooners like Charles Brown and Nat "King" Cole also maintained substantial audiences. And a blind, awesomely talented man named Ray Charles was rocketing into the public eye.

In short, there was plenty of music to choose from. Music writer Gerri Hirshey notes: "American kids were proving to be voracious consumers. They seemed born to seize and follow trends. At that time there was ample choice. . . . There was so much going on."[38]

All this variety created fertile possibilities for innovation. The 1960s was a decade of extraordinary social and political upheavals, and black popular music met the challenge. It was about to enter a major new phase, as a new style—soul music— came to the forefront.

Chapter Five

That Sweet Soul Music

The line dividing R&B and soul was never precise. Indeed, many musicians and fans simply ignored the distinction, as earlier they had ignored differences between R&B and rock and roll. To them, the only useful distinction—to paraphrase Duke Ellington—was between good music and bad music.

Nonetheless, some general characteristics defined soul over R&B. Overall, soul had a more serious and urgent edge; it was less happy-go-lucky. Musically, it was more adventuresome; composers used increasingly bold arrangements or unusual instrumentation. And, perhaps most importantly, the lyrics of soul music often—though not always—were powerful socio-political commentaries.

"Music with a Philosophy"

Previously, pop music of any type had rarely been more than entertainment. It was for dancing, for having a good time, or for drowning one's sorrows. Now, however, black pop gained a social conscience, because the music was closely associated with a major event in American history. This was the civil rights movement, in which black citizens struggled for equality in such arenas as voting rights, job opportunities, and education.

Nina Simone performs at the Newport Jazz Festival in Rhode Island in 1967.

Racial tensions ran high during this period, and pop songs reflected the volatile mood. They increasingly addressed potent issues of civil rights, as well as a related self-esteem movement that emphasized black pride. *Billboard* called such songs "music with a philosophy, black nationalism in pop."[39]

As did all black pop music, soul mingled sadness and joy. The civil rights movement had deep difficulties, serious disappointments, and very real battles. But the feeling of soul—"sweet soul music," to borrow a song title—was often positive, reflecting the hopeful nature of the struggle. Music scholar Peter Guralnick writes, "[Soul] was a peculiarly good-hearted and optimistic sort of music, and it is no accident that its popularity was limited to the early and middle Sixties, a time when awakening black pride went hand in hand with civil rights activism and racial progress seemed more real than illusory."[40]

Keeping Faith Alive

Many soul songs directly reflected the civil rights movement's issues. One was James Brown's "Say It Loud (I'm Black and I'm Proud)." Other examples included Curtis Mayfield and the Impressions' "We're a Winner" and "Keep On Pushing," Aretha Franklin's "Young, Gifted, and Black," Nina Simone's "Mississippi Goddamn," and Sam Cooke's "A Change Is Gonna Come."

Civil rights activists also adopted a number of old gospel songs for their cause. The connection between the movement and traditional gospel was natural. Civil rights activism was intimately connected with the African American church; both entities shared common themes of freedom, equality, unity, and peace, and many key civil rights leaders were also ministers.

Old spirituals, fitted with new words, were called freedom songs. Among the best known were "We Shall Overcome" and "Kumbaya." Such songs did much to lift the spirits of activists when they faced difficult times. The movement's most prominent leader, Dr. Martin Luther King Jr., noted that the songs provided "new courage and a sense of unity. . . . They keep alive a faith, a radiant hope in the future."[41]

The Genius

But soul music was not just serious songs about racial equality. Much of it—indeed, much of the best—covered the same topics that popular music had always covered: dancing and romancing, having a good time, and drowning in one's own tears.

One performer in particular rarely spoke out publicly on political issues, but must nonetheless head any list of soul giants. This was Ray Charles—the Genius of Soul, as he was known. Charles was a remarkable composer, pianist, and arranger, but the essence of his talent was his dazzling voice. Writing in 1988, jazz critic Whitney Balliett noted:

Ray Charles, pictured here in 1962, was known as the Genius of Soul.

Charles can sing anything short of lieder [classical art songs] and opera. . . . He can shape his baritone voice into dark, shouting blocks of sound, reduce it to a goose-pimpling whisper, sing in a pure falsetto, yodel, resemble Nat Cole at his creamiest, and growl and rasp. He is always surprising.[42]

Blind since his Florida childhood, Charles was a professional musician by fifteen and spent years on the road before achieving fame. Early on, Charles was a smooth pop crooner who idolized singers like Nat "King" Cole. But he found his own voice in the mid-1950s when Atlantic Records executives encouraged an original style that combined Charles's earthy vocals with rolling, gospel-drenched piano and a punchy horn section.

Charles's marriage of religious and popular music, shocking for the time, was not a new idea; he just did it more overtly, and better, than anyone else. Many of his songs were adapted from existing gospel songs; for example, "This Little Girl of Mine" started as "This Little Light of Mine." Charles scandalized many listeners, but he also perfectly expressed a recurring theme in soul music: the link between religious passion and sexual joy.

Charles first hit it big with "I've Got a Woman" and followed it with many others, including "Hallelujah, I Just Love Her So" and "Drown in My Own Tears." His songs changed the course of soul by establishing a gold standard of quality. Writer Joe Levy comments, "The hit records [Charles] made for Atlantic in the mid-50s mapped out everything that would happen to . . . soul music in the years that followed."[43]

"Piled Three Deep"

The ones most scandalized by Charles's mix of religious and sexual fervor were performers and fans of gospel. Many of these people banned nonreligious song—the "devil's music"—from their homes and flatly refused to perform it. Gospel virtuoso Shirley Caesar once declared, "The U.S.A. doesn't have enough money to make me sing rock'n'roll!"[44]

But the money and fame pop music could bring were tempting. Some singers cast an envious eye at Charles, whose mix of sacred music with pop made him a rich celebrity. And in the mid-1950s, an established gospel star crossed over.

Sam Cooke grew up in Chicago, the center of gospel music. As a teenager, he became the lead singer for one of gospel's top groups, the Soul Stirrers; blessed with a soaring voice, movie-star looks, and a charismatic stage presence, he became sacred music's first teen idol. Night after night, Cooke wrecked the house—drove audiences wild with joy—and in particular made female admirers swoon. Fellow singer Wilson Pickett admiringly noted:

"Them sisters fell out like dominoes when Sam took the lead. Bang. Flat-out. Piled three deep in the aisles."[45]

Cooke had ambitions far beyond gospel and had always loved jazz and blues, though he had to listen to them in secret from his disapproving family. He took the plunge into pop and hit it big in 1957 with "You Send Me." The gospel community was devastated, but millions of others loved his new direction. Cooke followed "You Send Me" with more smash hits, including "Cupid," "Bring It On Home to Me," "Wonderful World," and "Havin' a Party."

Countless others, following Cooke's example, at least partly abandoned gospel for careers in what was by then called soul. In addition to Pickett, they included such stellar performers as Johnny Adams, Lou Rawls, Dinah Washington, Johnny Taylor, Bobby Womack, and Irma Thomas.

Aretha Franklin's gospel background led to her phenomenal career as a soul singer.

The Queen

All were abundantly talented, but perhaps the most gifted of all was Aretha Franklin. Even in such a crowded field, Franklin's voice was without parallel. She fully earned her nicknames: Lady Soul and the Queen of Soul.

Franklin was born into gospel royalty; her father, Reverend C.L. Franklin, was a minister in Detroit with a national reputation for his stirring sermons, and as a child Aretha sang in his choir. Her first attempts at recording pop failed, but then Atlantic Records, as it had with Ray Charles, nurtured her gospel roots.

Franklin's producer, Jerry Wexler—the same man who had coined the phrase "rhythm and blues"—recalls that his recording method was simple: "I took her to church, sat her down at the piano, let her be herself."[46]

The results paid off brilliantly. Franklin's first Atlantic single, "I Never Loved a Man," sold a million within weeks and was followed by such now-classics as "Respect," "Chain of Fools," "(You Make Me Feel Like a) Natural Woman," and "Do Right Woman." Each was marked by Franklin's hair-raising, powerfully honest voice; Peter Guralnick asserts, "There has been no pop singer more inspired than Aretha when it comes to sheer vocal artistry."[47]

The Godfather

The fourth key individual in the birth of soul was James Brown— also known as the Hardest-Working Man in Show Business, Mr. Dynamite, the Godfather of Soul, and Soul Brother Number One. Brown's music was an unlikely hit; his voice was abrasive and rough-hewn, the very opposite of a smooth, commercial sound. But his chief contribution to the music, a brilliant use of rhythm, made him a star and an icon.

Brown had a difficult childhood in Georgia, drifted into a life of crime, and was imprisoned at the age of sixteen for car theft. After his release, he joined a gospel quartet that became an R&B group. Soon, he was the leader, and its name became James Brown and the Famous Flames.

This group morphed into the legendary James Brown Revue. The revue's core was a top-flight band, the JBs, that specialized in laying down extended, tight, polyrhythmic grooves. There were almost no chord changes in Brown's songs; they depended entirely on rhythm for their forward movement.

Virtually every instrument became percussion. Guitars scratched out rhythms, horns provided rapid-fire bursts, and basses stressed the "one" (the first beat of the measure). Over this carpet of rhythm, Brown's singing, grunts, moans, and shouts soared with the fire of a Baptist minister. And then there was his astonishing dancing, as precise and swift as his singing. According to legend, Brown sweated away seven pounds at every show.

His many hit singles included "I Feel Good," "Please Please Please," and "Papa's Got a Brand New Bag." But Brown's extend-

---

A Magic Quilt

■

In James Brown's mighty band, as in traditional African music, rhythm was everything, and his musicians learned to watch carefully for subtle hand and body gestures from their leader signaling rhythmic changes. In fact, they were docked pay if they missed one of these cues. According to Brown's longtime road manager, Alan Leeds, the net effect of this careful study was a complex musical patchwork: "So the magic became something like putting a quilt together—taking all the rhythm patterns and weaving them in such a magical way as to create this wonderful *feel* that's going to drive audiences crazy."

Quoted in Robert Palmer, *Rock and Roll: An Unruly History.* New York: Harmony, 1995, p. 243.

---

ed grooves were not designed for three-minute records; his magic was in live shows best captured on LPs. One of these, 1963's *Live at the Apollo*, spent an amazing sixty-six weeks on the *Billboard* chart. Brown's fame increased over the years, and by 1971 he claimed to be the highest-paid black entertainer in the world.

Motown

Individuals like Brown were not the only musicians to forge signature sounds. During the soul years, two record labels, Motown and Stax, stood out by becoming brand names with distinctive, exciting sounds.

Motown Records was named for the location of its headquarters: Detroit, the Motor City. Started on a shoestring, Motown became one of the most successful black-owned music organizations in history. Along the way, not coincidentally, it made some unforgettable pop music.

Its founder was Berry Gordy. Gordy was lucky in his choice of musical partners: William "Smokey" Robinson, a songwriter, producer, and the lead singer of the Miracles. Robinson's creamy voice melted hearts, and his brilliantly simple songs led Bob Dylan to call him "America's greatest living poet."[48]

James Brown, known as the Godfather of Soul, performs for American troops during the Vietnam War in 1968.

Together with a gifted crew of associates, Gordy and Robinson created the signature Motown sound. Its catchy melodies, danceable beats, easily grasped lyrics, and strong vocals were carefully crafted to appeal to a broad range of listeners. The sound was instantly recognizable, even on tinny car radios or transistor radios; as the legendary pop producer Phil Spector once remarked, "You put on a Motown record and it jumps at you."[49]

The Hit Factory

Borrowing the streamlining principle of Detroit's automobile factories, Gordy created an assembly line for his performers, with professionals completing specific functions at every step. A house band created the backing music. Experts crafted stage outfits and dance steps. Accountants kept careful control of money, doling out modest allowances. There was even a charm school, where singers learned to act on- and offstage with grace.

The results of this meticulous work were immediate and stunning. Even before the company's operations were finalized, the hits started coming. Kempton notes, "Motown put six records at the top of the pop charts before its bookkeepers had a systematic way of accounting for all the money it routinely advanced to the singers who made them."[50]

Not every Motown release was a smash, but its overall success rate was amazing. During the 1960s, most labels celebrated if 10 percent of their releases made the Top 100 on the sales charts; Motown's average was 65 percent. Among its most consistent stars were the Miracles, the Marvelettes, Marvin Gaye, Mary Wells, Martha and the Vandellas, the Four Tops, and the Temptations. A blind child prodigy, "Little" Stevie Wonder, had his first hits during this period, while Diana Ross and the Supremes scored an astonishing twelve number one records within five years.

Stax

Meanwhile, a very different but equally influential label was developing in Memphis. This sultry city already had a long history as a center for blues and R&B. Now it nurtured one of the most exciting strains of soul: the tough, earthy sounds of Stax. Like Motown, Stax was a consistent brand; to use an expression just coming into general musical use, a Stax record was always funky.

Also like Motown, Stax began on a shoestring, operating out of an old theater on a variety of ancient recording machines. Another similarity was its regular stable of gifted in-house producers, writers, singers, and musicians.

"Just a Bunch of Kids"

■

Motown Records artists were kept on strict allowances, with the company doling out only a small portion of their earnings and keeping the rest in trust. In return, company president Berry Gordy expected achievement, hard work, trust, and loyalty. To a high degree, he got it. Being part of the Motown family, singer Mary Wells recalls, was both fun and educational: "We were all kids . . . just a bunch of kids that cared about each other, just havin' fun. Growin' up together. . . . Those were our years of higher education."

Quoted in Gerri Hirshey, *Nowhere to Run: The Story of Soul Music.* New York: Times, 1984, p. 143.

Unlike Motown, however, Stax was a notably biracial organization—an unusual situation during this period of simmering racial tension nationwide. The label's owners were white; its producers, engineers, and musicians were racially mixed. Among its most frequently used backing musicians, for instance, were Booker T. and the MGs and the Memphis Horns; both groups were integrated.

"You Know Exactly"

Stax's featured artists, meanwhile, were primarily black, each possessed of a distinctive voice and style. Among the most successful were Sam and Dave ("Soothe Me," "Soul Man"), Carla Thomas ("Gee Whiz"), and Wilson Pickett ("In the Midnight Hour"). Stax was also home to Otis Redding, whose voice blended the silky charm of Sam Cooke with the urgency of James Brown.

Otis Redding, famous for his song "(Sittin' on) the Dock of the Bay," had success as a singer and a songwriter.

Redding was also a gifted songwriter, responsible for such hits as "Respect" (famously recorded by Aretha Franklin), "I've Been Loving You Too Long," and "(Sittin' on) the Dock of the Bay." Tragically, the singer's career ended in 1967 when he and several band members died in an airplane crash. MGs guitarist Steve Cropper summed up Redding's appeal in a comment that could apply to all soul music: "He gets over to the people what he's talking about, and he does it in so few words that if you read them on paper they might not make any sense. But when you hear the way he sings them, you know exactly what he is talking about."[51]

The Blues Revival

The singers of Stax and Motown—and countless other soul artists—defined the bulk of black pop music in the early and mid-1960s. However, these years were not a fertile time for a style that had profoundly influenced soul. The blues was generally ignored until a surprising development took place. This was the British Invasion, a wave of English pop musicians that swept the United States in the wake of the Beatles' 1964 appearances.

The Invasion bands typically modeled themselves on American blues and R&B artists. The Rolling Stones named themselves after a Muddy Waters song. Pete Townshend, the Who's guitarist, idolized Steve Cropper. The Beatles worshipped Fats Domino and Chuck Berry. And the list went on; Ahmet Ertegun, a founder of Atlantic Records, remarks, "Clyde McPhatter and the Drifters and Ray Charles, Chuck Berry and so on [were] the models that the Beatles and the Rolling Stones used to form their own music."[52]

Most of these bands, suddenly famous among teenaged whites, were happy to acknowledge their musical debt to black America. This sparked a resurgence of interest in the blues; Muddy Waters and Howlin' Wolf were among the performers whose careers were thus boosted. Many African Americans were upset that white musicians were once again hogging the limelight; nonetheless, the attention from overseas did much to revive a classic form of black music.

End of an Era

The blues revival and the soul movement did not last. In particular, the end of soul was tied to that of the civil rights movement. The main period of that movement ended, in the opinion of many historians, with the assassination of Martin Luther King Jr. in 1968. Not coincidentally, classic soul began to wane at the same time.

The next period—the late 1960s and 1970s—was as volatile in America as the civil rights era had been. It was a different time, however—less optimistic, more conflicted. The course of black music reflected this uncertainty; the music was changing yet again.

Chapter Six

Dancing the Seventies Away

The late 1960s and 1970s were mixed years for black pop music, reflecting the state of American society. This period of turmoil and upheaval saw massive protests against the Vietnam War and armed militancy in place of the civil rights era's nonviolent protests. The era was symbolized by the bitter slogan "Burn, baby, burn"—a reference to the fiery riots that frequently came from race-related confrontations.

Reflecting this turmoil, the overall music scene fractured, creating several distinct genres, and black pop followed this trend. Much of the era's black pop was a direct extension of soul's serious, socially conscious music. But there was also a strong streak of escapism; times were tough, and many people simply wanted some decent party music.

No matter what form it took, virtually all of the African American pop of the era had one thing in common: It was good to dance to. The late 1960s and 1970s were, if nothing else, great years for dancing.

Are You Experienced?

One major black musician of the late 1960s and early 1970s was, paradoxically, associated with white music. By this time, rock and roll had become simply rock—the dominant form of popular music in the world, listened to mainly by white teens and young adults. Only a handful of black musicians were out-and-out rockers, and, it can be argued, black music significantly intersected rock in only one place during this period: in the person of Jimi Hendrix.

Born and raised in Seattle, Hendrix cut his teeth as a blues/R&B guitarist and singer with a reputation for a showy stage manner. In 1966, increasingly influenced by rock, he moved to London and formed a trio with two white Britons. The Jimi Hendrix Experience played ferocious, shockingly loud rock with a strong foundation of electric blues. Its incendiary leader, a sensation in Europe, became an instant legend in the United States after his appearance at an outdoor festival in Monterey, California, in 1967.

Jimi Hendrix performs at a concert in 1967. His music combined rock and roll with elements of the blues.

Hendrix died just three years later, in 1970—the victim of a drug overdose, probably accidental. But the records he made during his brief career, including *Are You Experienced?* and *Electric Ladyland*, have inspired countless guitarists since; Hendrix's fiery style, always testing the boundaries of what a guitar could do, created a legacy that many feel has yet to be equaled. Rock critic John Morthland argues, "None has actually extended the directions he pursued, but perhaps that is because he took them, in his painfully short time on earth, as far as they could go."[53]

Sly and Marvin

Hendrix's music was revolutionary in a musical sense, but it was not often overtly political. Many other black performers were outspoken on issues of the day, however. One such influential figure was Sly Stone, a keyboardist, singer, and songwriter from the San Francisco Bay Area.

Stone's earliest hits, such as "Everyday People," were dance tunes with relatively mild social commentary. Stone's music became increasingly political, however, and his controversial 1971 album, *There's a Riot Goin' On*, used disjointed music and bold lyrics to address such subjects as violence, drug abuse, and armed revolution. By today's standard, the album seems tame, but at the time its radical nature caused an uproar.

Another musician to mix social commentary with music was Marvin Gaye, a longtime star in the Motown universe. His 1971 release, *What's Goin' On*, included songs that frankly addressed issues of the day, such as the title track, as well as "Mercy Mercy

Sly and the Family Stone put on an amazing performance in San Francisco, California, in 1969.

Stevie Wonder's long career began when he was a teenager. Here he performs at a concert in the 1970s.

Me (the Ecology)," and "Inner City Blues." The album was much bolder, politically, than anything Motown had ever done.

Motown chief Berry Gordy generally disliked overtly political music, and at first refused to release *What's Goin' On.* Gaye insisted, however; music critic Robert Palmer writes: "Marvin Gaye saw 'pushing the envelope' as both a privilege and a duty: This was what being an artist was all about."[54] Gaye's faith was justified; *What's Goin' On* was a huge success with the listening public and became one of Motown's all-time biggest sellers.

Stevie Grows Up

Gaye's success with *What's Goin' On* helped give another Motown star a similar state of artistic freedom. Stevie Wonder, equally gifted as a songwriter, singer, musician, and producer, became famous before he reached his teens. But Motown strictly controlled every aspect of his professional life, from publishing and production to tour schedules and income. It has been estimated that by 1970 the singer had earned over $30 million for Motown—but had received only $1 million of that.

When Wonder turned twenty-one in 1971, he was able to negotiate a new contract with Motown. The result was millions of dollars in back royalties, along with complete artistic control. Announcing that he was "not interested in 'baby, baby' songs any more,"[55] Wonder used his new freedom to create some of the most innovative and significant recordings in popular music.

Wonder's releases during this time, his golden years, included *Music of My Mind, Talking Book, Innervisions,* and *Songs in the Key of Life.* Some of his songs, such as "Isn't She Lovely" and "You Are the Sunshine of My Life," extended Wonder's ongoing line of brilliantly melodic songs about love and family. Others, such as "Livin' for the City," reflected the singer's growing concern with social, political, and spiritual issues. In either case, Wonder's deep, widespread influence on pop music—touching virtually every aspect of singing, writing, playing, and production—would continue for decades.

Soul Man

Gaye and Wonder were always closely associated with Detroit, but considerable musical innovation was going on elsewhere as well. In Memphis, for example, Stax producer Isaac Hayes created such groundbreaking albums as *Hot Buttered Soul* and the sound track album for *Shaft,* the quintessential blaxploitation inner-city adventure movie.

But Memphis was perhaps best represented during the 1970s by singer Al Green. Like so many other black musicians, Green got his start in church. He later recalled of the gospel he heard during his Arkansas childhood: "It was put in my cornbread. . . . My mother and my father, they were Baptists. We were raised in the church, and we sang at home. I started when I was just a little peewee. I was just raised on the sound of Sam Cooke and the Soul Stirrers and the whole trip."[56]

Green sang in church choirs and with his siblings. But he also loved blues and R&B, hiding this enthusiasm from his family. When his secret was discovered, Green struck out on his own and found success when he met Willie Mitchell, a producer and bandleader with whom he clicked stylistically.

Green combined his own compositions with Mitchell's sturdy production, which merged a rock-solid core band with sparse horns and strings. Riding above it all was Green's unmistakable singing—a brilliant instrument that, like Ray Charles's very different voice, took many shapes. Green could make it a supple falsetto, a breathless romantic croon, or a shout with the authority of a Sunday preacher.

The result made him the decade's top Soul Man, responsible for such classics as "I'm So Tired of Being Alone," "I'm Still in Love with You," and "Call Me." Then, at the height of his popularity, Green experienced a spiritual reawakening; he became a minister, parted ways with Mitchell, and turned his back on the commercial music industry. He kept recording,

Al Green's soul and gospel songs showcased his versatile voice.

however, developing a smooth, intimate, semiacoustic sound for the gospel music he sang over the next several decades.

The Sound of Philadelphia

Another distinctive 1970s style emerged from Philadelphia. This was a brand of infectious dance music called the Philly Sound. According to writer Kevin Phinney, the genre "defined soul music in the early 1970s."[57]

Philadelphia International (PI), the label behind the Philly Sound, was phenomenally successful, second only to Motown as a black-owned record company. Among PI's most successful artists were the O'Jays, Harold Melvin and the Blue Notes, the Spinners, and Billy Paul. The label's chief architects, meanwhile, were songwriters and producers Leon Huff, Kenny Gamble, and Thom Bell.

They created a sound that was smooth, commercial, and heavily orchestrated, but also very funky. Lyrically, PI records tended toward the inspirational. The Philly Sound was thus a hybrid; it was great for dancing—but also, popular culture professor Mark Anthony Neal notes, it dealt frankly with such weighty subjects as "communal [shared] values, black-on-black crime, interclass relations, and the diminishing quality of both black public and private life."[58]

Disco

The Philly Sound, appealing strongly to dance fans, formed a crucial link between the dance-and-romance soul of the 1960s and a style that had a short but forceful reign in the mid-1970s. This was disco, a genre that, for better or worse, epitomizes the decade for many.

Disco's roots can be traced to black dance clubs of the 1950s, where people danced to records instead of live bands. In the 1960s, a European fad for these discotheques briefly swept the United States. Celebrities like First Lady Jackie Kennedy could be seen performing the latest dance steps in fashionable discotheques. In the early 1970s, similar dance clubs reappeared in New York. Now called discos, they were associated with the city's gay, Latino, and black subcultures.

Instead of a live band, a DJ provided music at a disco; his (or, rarely, her) job was to use the hottest records to provide a sound track for nonstop dancing. Disco was emphatically nonpolitical, caring about nothing but the boogie, and musically it could not have been simpler. Its basis was a relentless, pounding rhythm that stressed every beat. Anything could then be laid on top, from soulful vocals and Mozart melodies to wiggling synthesizer figures or screaming guitars.

Disco Spreads

For some time, disco and its culture remained underground. However, it eventually spread to the mainstream, expanding far beyond its original audience and making stars of a number of singers and groups, black and white alike. Among these were Donna Summer, Gloria Gaynor, Barry White, Kool & the Gang, Abba, and the Village People, a cartoonish group that parodied gay stereotypes.

As the fad spread, many established artists from other genres —including Rod Stewart, the Beach Boys, the Rolling Stones, and even Frank Sinatra and Barbra Streisand—dabbled in disco.

"Dance-Floor Anthems"

Kenny Gamble and Leon Huff were the primary forces behind the Philly Sound, a heavily orchestrated dance style of the early 1970s that served as a bridge between disco and earlier dance styles. While the music was strictly dance oriented, the lyrics of typical Philly Sound songs were uplifting and inspirational. Mark Anthony Neal notes:

> While producers of black popular music in past eras correctly understood the role of the black church as the dominant [force in the African American community], Gamble and Huff understood the role of the dance floor in the maintenance of black communal relations. Harking back to the 1930s and 1940s, [they] created dance-floor anthems [that] affirmed black communal and familial relations.

Club-goers dance the night away at a disco in Detroit, Michigan, in 1978.

Mark Anthony Neal, *What the Music Said: Black Popular Music and Black Popular Culture.* New York: Routledge, 1999, pp. 119–20.

The Bee Gees show off their Grammy for Best Album, *Saturday Night Fever*, in 1979.

Far and away the most successful were the Bee Gees, who supplied some of the sound track music for *Saturday Night Fever*, a monstrously popular disco film starring John Travolta.

The glitzy disco lifestyle, with its emphasis on drugs, glamour, and questionable fashion choices, faded after a few years, and so did the music. In its day, however, disco was a potent force. If nothing else, it provoked strong reactions of love or hate among music fans; writer Mikal Gilmore notes that disco was "one of the most popular and reviled mileposts in pop music's history."[59]

Funk

As disco waned in the late 1970s, another style emerged. This was funk, a less polished genre that developed, at least in part, as a backlash to the glossiness of disco.

Funk had clear roots in earlier genres. For example, it prominently used James Brown's method of combining multiple rhythms, staccato horns, and heavy bass lines emphasizing the first beat of every measure. Funk also used elements of hard rock, especially screaming, Hendrix-like guitars and wild keyboards borrowed from Sly Stone. And it incorporated newer elements, like the recently invented synthesizer. This melding of past and present was quite conscious, writer Ken Tucker notes: "Disco wanted you to think that [it] had been invented yesterday [but funk] wanted you to know it had a past."[60]

The prominence of a melodic bass in funk was symbolized by the fact that two of its foremost bandleaders were also bassists. Larry Graham played with Sly Stone for years before forming

Graham Central Station; Bootsy Collins played with James Brown before creating Bootsy's Rubber Band. Among the many other prominent funk bands were the Ohio Players, Tower of Power, and Earth, Wind, and Fire.

P-Funk

All of these bands were distinctive, but, for many fans, funk found its highest expression in a wild and wild-haired visionary, George Clinton. Clinton was the mad-genius leader of two overlapping groups, Parliament and Funkadelic. This extended family of musicians was referred to as P-Funk, and among its many albums were the hugely popular *Chocolate City* and *One Nation Under a Groove*.

Clinton was a former Motown songwriter. He intimately knew and disapproved of the company's assembly line attitude about

---

Funk Music as a Melting Pot

◼

Funk music, to a higher degree than most other styles, mixed it up racially. One of funk's direct ancestors, Sly Stone, fronted a multiracial band. And one of the top funk bands of the 1970s, Tower of Power, featured both black and white vocalists and instrumental horn soloists. Writer Kevin Phinney comments:

> Black performers fuzzed up the bass and freaked out on guitar. White rockers challenged the limits of rhythmic elasticity, and once inviolable dictums of formatted radio chipped away like so much old paint. Divisions in race and music dissolved, and it seemed to be only a matter of time before the new contagion of brotherly love filtered out into society at large. It was America-as-Melting-Pot, wrestled into a mind-blowing variety of styles and sounds that couldn't easily be catalogued according to race.

Kevin Phinney, *Souled American: How Black Music Transformed White Culture*. New York: Billboard, 2005, p. 242.

One of funk music's most famous artists, George Clinton, performs with his group Funkadelic in 1978.

music. He was drawn instead to performers like Brown and Hendrix, mavericks who went outside established boundaries to forge their own idiosyncratic styles.

Clinton succeeded brilliantly in creating his own style. A single P-Funk song might include Hendrix-style guitar freak-outs, complex polyrhythms, jazzy horns, old-fashioned harmony vocals, and space-age electronics. P-Funk's live shows, meanwhile, featured bizarre costumes and complex, often silly stage effects—such as a giant, saucer-shaped "mothership" from which the musicians emerged. Music writer Joe McEwen notes that this "mixture of tribal funk, elaborate stage props and the relentless assault on personal inhibition resembled nothing so much as a Space Age Mardi Gras."[61]

Holding it all together was Clinton's philosophy, which mixed racial pride with cosmic science fiction, sexual liberation, mythology, and more. Overall, P-Funk was great fun, but it also contained a serious message. Mark Anthony Neal notes, "Under-lying much of the surface imagery of Parliament/Funkadelic were sharp critiques of mass culture, particularly within the realms of black popular music, and black nationalist rhetoric."[62]

Quiet Storm

Of course, not all 1970s black pop music was mindless disco or raucous funk. For example, one movement focused on extending traditional romantic aspects of R&B. Introspective love songs, with an emphasis on a smooth and highly commercial sound, were especially popular.

The late 1970s version of this evergreen style was called Quiet Storm, after a 1975 Smokey Robinson album. The Quiet Storm genre became popular enough that many radio stations adopted it as a specific format—a mixture of soulful ballads, easygoing jazz, and a little blues. Robinson, Teddy Pendergrass, Patti Labelle, Peabo Bryson, Anita Baker, and Roberta Flack were among the most prominent exponents of this mellow style.

But, as usual, the styles of the 1970s did not last long. Toward the end of the decade, the beginnings of another major shift began. Black pop music once again started to change as the decade faded into the 1980s.

Chapter Seven

The Beats Go On

The most significant development in black pop music during the 1980s was the explosive rise and mass acceptance of hip-hop and rap. This music radically de-emphasized melody and harmony, stripping away virtually everything except rhythmic beats and spoken, or rapped, vocals. (Originally, the term *hip-hop* referred to the entire lifestyle the music represented, *rap* to a spoken vocal. Over time, however, *rap* and *hip-hop* have become more or less interchangeable.)

Besides the radical downplaying of melody, rap had unusual instrumentation. It did not use conventional instruments, relying instead on record turntables and drum machines to create rhythms. In time, rap also incorporated more sophisticated technology, such as sampling—repeating small bits of already familiar songs for rhythmic effect.

As with earlier musical movements, such as bebop, hip-hop developed far from the mainstream, as a rebellion against traditional styles. Also like bebop, hip-hop was part of an entire urban lifestyle that embraced specific, ever-changing fashions, dance styles, slang, and art. These things helped define the hip-hop community and separate it from the mainstream.

DJ Kool Herc

Hip-hop began in the New York City borough of the Bronx in the late 1970s. Using massive sound systems, a group of young disc jockeys from Jamaica played dance records for parties. One of these was DJ Kool Herc (real name: Clive Campbell), today acknowledged as the music's primary innovator. He recalls: "It's funny, because, at the time, I never thought of myself as creating a new form of music. I just wanted to see people having fun."[63]

Herc's innovation came when he noticed that dancers enjoyed certain moments in records more than others. Everyone wanted these breaks—brief segments when everything but the percussion dropped out—to last as long as possible. Herc found he could sustain a break indefinitely by using two turntables and two copies of the same record, cutting quickly back and forth between the two.

DJ Kool Herc, pictured here at a 2006 news conference, pioneered the use of playing records on two turntables at the same time.

Herc sometimes augmented the breaks' steady beats by adding words spoken over microphones, often by two or more people. This was similar to toasting, a tradition from Jamaica in which DJs talked in rapid-fire, semi-improvised rhyme, over music. Similar practices appear elsewhere in black musical history, and in fact the tradition can be traced back to the griots (poets) of Africa.

The First Rap Records

Younger musicians, such as Afrika Bambaataa, Grandmaster Theodore, and the Cold

The Roots of Rap

In this passage, music professor Guthrie P. Ramsey Jr. comments on the deep roots of rap:

> The idea of rapping has deep roots in African American culture. Its stylistic and thematic predecessors are numerous: the dozens and toasting traditions from America and Jamaica; sing-song children's games; double-dutch chants; black vernacular preaching styles; the jazz vocalese of King Pleasure, Eddie Jefferson, and Oscar Brown, Jr.; the on-the-air verbal virtuosity of black DJs; scat singing; courtship rituals; the lovers' raps of Isaac Hayes, Barry White, and Millie Jackson; the politicized storytelling of Gil Scott-Heron and the Last Poets; and the preacherly vocables of Ray Charles, James Brown, and George Clinton, among many others.

Guthrie P. Ramsey Jr., *Race Music: Black Cultures from Bebop to Hip-Hop.* Berkeley and Los Angeles: University of California Press, 2003, p. 165.

Crush Brothers, modified Herc's basic ideas. Some added sung vocals over the beat. Others experimented with scratching, manually moving a record back and forth on a turntable to produce rhythms, or used a beat box, an electronic drum machine.

Gradually, MCs (masters of ceremonies or microphone controllers) took equal space in the spotlight along with DJs, who were also called mixers. MCs spoke directly to the audience. Over the DJs' rhythms, they created rapid-fire shout outs, or greetings to specific people, as well as raps in which they boasted about themselves or teased other rappers.

The style took shape within a context of social strife. The poorer neighborhoods of New York in the 1970s could be frightening and dangerous—rife with crime, gangs, and drugs. For young African Americans and Latinos drawn to the hip-hop scene, the music—which often had positive, uplifting themes—was their response to this environment. According to music writer Nelson George, hip-hop was "a child that walked, talked, and partied amid negativity."[64]

The "Dollar Bill Disease"

The style stayed underground for some time. Its creators remained local, and their only recordings were homemade cassette tapes that circulated around the Bronx and nearby neighborhoods. Although later rap would become associated with money and violence, the music in these early days was mostly about fashion and good-natured competition between groups. Writer Michael A. Gonzales notes, "In the days before the 'dollar bill disease' . . . the competitions . . . were the dividing-line factor between the merely good and being the best in the eyes of the hood."[65]

In 1979, the first rap records came out: "King Tim III," by the Fatback Band, and a surprise hit, "Rapper's Delight," by the Sugar Hill Gang. In 1982 came "The Message" by Grandmaster Flash and the Furious Five. Mark Anthony Neal notes that this song earned critical attention for its blunt comments, perceived by the listening public as genuine, about the struggles of inner-city life: "Part of the recording's obvious appeal to mainstream critics was

The Sugar Hill Gang poses backstage during Grammy Fest 2003. The group released one of rap music's first records, "Rapper's Delight," in 1979.

its unmitigated [pure] and 'authentic' portrayal of contemporary black urban life."[66]

Hip-hop began to spread, with small enclaves of performers and fans developing across the country. Its popularity took a huge jump in the mid-1980s with *Raising Hell*, an album by Run-DMC that had notably aggressive lyrics and music. A highlight was "Walk This Way," Run-DMC's collaboration with members of the white rock band Aerosmith. The song's clever video showed the groups on opposite sides of a wall, playing different versions and maddening each other—then tearing down the wall and jamming together.

Exploding

"Walk This Way" appealed powerfully to white rockers and black hip-hoppers alike; it helped bring rap to a wider, mainstream audience, and the genre's popularity exploded in the following years. Rapper Kurtis Blow appeared in a soft drink commercial, MTV started a popular show called *Yo! MTV Raps*, and performers like LL Cool J and Slick Rick scored major hits. The music's presence in the mainstream was cemented when the first Grammy Award for rap was given in 1988 to a pop-oriented duo, DJ Jazzy Jeff and the Fresh Prince (Will Smith).

Many rap pioneers deplored this massive popularity as selling out. They complained that the music no longer belonged to a select few, that it was being diluted for a wider audience. Russell Simmons, cofounder of the record label Def Jam, said of the move to the mainstream: "Hip-hop didn't cross over from black to white. It crossed over from cool to uncool."[67]

On the other hand, the move to the mainstream can be seen as a natural progression of events for any musical style. Nelson George comments: "Twenty-first century hip-hop is an industry with institutions, orthodoxies, and dogmas. That's cool. That's evolution. That's life."[68]

East vs. West

As its popularity increased, rap split into several factions. One was relatively tame and commercial, represented by such musicians as the Fresh Prince and MC Hammer. Otherwise, rap was roughly divided into two camps, centered on the West and East Coasts.

MJ and MTV

In the early 1980s, Michael Jackson was the first African American artist to benefit significantly from an exciting new phenomenon in popular music: the music video. Previously, MTV, the cable channel that introduced videos to the world, had focused on reaching young white rock fans and so had virtually ignored black artists. Of the 750 videos shown in the network's first year and a half, fewer than two dozen featured black musicians.

Jackson virtually destroyed racial barriers on the channel with videos like those accompanying his songs "Billie Jean" and "Thriller." They succeeded because they were visually compelling. Jackson was a brilliant dancer, and his visual appeal was just as strong as his music. In addition, his production values were far beyond anything previously seen on MTV. Jackson's videos, elaborate and professionally produced, set high standards for future work in the medium.

Speaking broadly, East Coast rap stressed social, spiritual, and political awareness, urging its listeners to study history and current issues. Public Enemy's thought-provoking *It Takes a Nation of Millions to Hold Us Back* typified this approach. Other East Coast rappers included the Fugees, who combined catchy pop with politics, and the Wu-Tang Clan, who mixed street-style rapping with references to Islam and kung fu. Not every New York rapper believed in using the music to further political awareness. For instance, Sean ("Puff Daddy" or "P. Diddy") Combs pioneered the use of a successful rap career as a springboard to running a massive retail empire.

West Coast rap, meanwhile, generally focused more on material possessions—money, clothes, and fancy cars. It also reflected aspects of the gangsta life—the inner-city black lifestyle, with its ongoing problems of poverty, neglect, drug abuse, violence, and crime. Among the chief exponents of West Coast rap were Ice-T and NWA, whose album *Straight Outta Compton* was the first

West Coast rappers NWA released the music industry's first mainstream gangsta album *Straight Outta Compton* in 1988.

mainstream gangsta album. Following NWA's breakup in 1992, several members pursued solo careers; among them was Dr. Dre, whose highly influential *The Chronic* introduced G Funk, a style that came to dominate West Coast rap by mixing funky beats with laid-back, drawling vocals.

Fueled in part by the media, a rivalry between East and West Coast rappers developed during the 1990s. Rivalries had long existed in the world of hip-hop but were often no more serious than the good-natured competitions between sports teams. However, the violent antagonism depicted in 1990s rap sometimes turned real. This apparently resulted in, among other tragedies, the still unsolved murders of two top performers, Tupac Shakur and the Notorious B.I.G.

Controversy

Violence is just one of rap's qualities to cause controversy. Critics also accuse rap of promoting the glorification of material goods, racism, and misogyny (antiwomen sentiments). Tipper Gore, the wife of former Vice President Al Gore, was a key activist in one method critics used: the creation of advisory stickers for explicit albums.

Rap is not the first African American music to be controversial; it is simply the latest. Journalist Christopher John Farley points out, "All major modern musical forms with roots in the black community—jazz, rock, even gospel—faced criticism early on."[69] And defenders of rap point out that it is a powerful method of communicating current ideas.

These fans note that rap is a flexible means of communication, adaptable for many situations and messages. As such, it connects communities that might otherwise be isolated, instantly bringing them news, ideas, and information. Chuck D, formerly of Public Enemy, has famously referred to rap as "black America's CNN."[70]

Widening Its Scope

Over the years, the scope of rap has widened considerably. For example, although its practitioners were once almost exclusively male, a number of important women rappers have emerged. They range from the first woman to make a solo rap record (Lady B.

Big Boi (left) and Andre 3000 (right) of OutKast perform at the Soul Train Music Awards in Los Angeles, California, in 2004.

and her "To the Beat, Y'all" in 1980) to such artists as Salt-N-Pepa, Lil' Kim, Missy Elliott, and Queen Latifah. A handful of significant white rappers have also emerged, including the Beastie Boys and the phenomenally successful Eminem.

Meanwhile, rap has created a dizzying number of stylistic subgenres and variations. Some of these have strong regional flavors. For example, OutKast, of Atlanta, Georgia, became hugely popular with a distinctively southern style incorporating a rhythm called southern bounce. Miami bass and crunk are two more styles that emerged from the South. Go-go, house, electro, and techno are still more spin-offs from hip-hop that have gained favor at various times.

Hip-hop has spread far beyond the boundaries of the United States. Musicians around the world have adopted it, leading to the phenomenon of rappers performing in a dizzying variety of languages. It has also led to fusions between hip-hop and native musical styles, from the Dominican Republic's merenrap, a blend of hip-hop and merengue rhythms, to Bongo Flava, Tanzania's version of the music.

And rap continues to evolve. Performers like Kanye West, Gnarls Barkley, Jay-Z, and 50 Cent consistently push the boundaries of the music, and new artists emerge every day. Rap remains an integral part of American popular culture, the current dominant style of black music, and a powerful influence on music worldwide.

1980s Mainstream

Of course, not everything in black pop from the 1980s to the present took place in the world of hip-hop. Many talented musicians were exploring other aspects of the music. Some of them were easy-to-take, traditional pop singers like Lionel Richie, Jeffrey Osbourne, and Whitney Houston. Others had more individual styles; for example, Prince fused such elements as Hendrix-style guitar, punk rock, soul, and funk to create his own eccentric and distinctive music.

But the biggest mainstream figure of the 1980s—indeed, a genuine pop culture phenomenon—was Michael Jackson. Jackson's family group, the Jackson Five, had been the last major act produced by Motown in the company's heyday. The preadolescent Michael's virtuoso singing and dancing made the Jackson Five one of the label's most enduringly popular groups.

Not until he went solo, however, did Jackson's career really explode. He and producer Quincy Jones struck gold with *Off the Wall* and, especially, *Thriller*. *Thriller* included collaborations with such disparate musicians as Paul McCartney and Eddie Van Halen, picked up a raft of Grammy Awards, remained in the Top Ten for over a year, and became the second best-selling album in history. (The first is the Eagles' *Their Greatest Hits, 1971–1975*.) Its runaway success earned Jackson the title King of Pop and made him a household name; music critic Paul Friedlander commented that with it Jackson achieved "one of the defining popular music moments of the eighties."[71]

New Jack Swing and More

More recently, mainstream black pop music has increasingly mixed classic soul and R&B with hip-hop. Indeed, there has been little recorded black pop in recent years that has not been influenced at least somewhat by hip-hop. One example was the movement called new jack swing.

Also known as swingbeat, new jack swing was succeeded by a style called nusoul. The genre mixes the vocal traditions of classic romantic R&B and soul with contemporary rhythms. This has created one of the strongest fusions of pop with R&B since the days of Motown.

Often, entirely new melodies and arrangements have been created. Sometimes, however, the music borrows existing songs, sampling riffs and figures from classic R&B or soul tunes and grafting them to

Michael Jackson performs in concert in 1984. Jackson's *Thriller* was released that year and went on to become the second best-selling album of all time.

hip-hop beats. Among key producers and performers in this style are L.A., Babyface, Teddy Riley, New Edition, Boyz II Men, Jodeci, Destiny's Child, R. Kelly, Toni Braxton, TLC, Mary J. Blige, D'Angelo, Usher, and Alicia Keys.

Hip-hop has also influenced the gospel music being created today. A new genre, broadly called contemporary gospel, seeks to combine the spiritual messages of traditional sacred music with modern beats. Among its most gifted performers are Kirk Franklin, Donnie McClurkin, and Yolanda Adams.

These artists strive to make gospel's sound current without compromising its ancient religious messages. Adams, recalling her early apprenticeship with Houston's Southeast Inspirational Choir, comments: "We were trying to make sure young people enjoyed gospel music, so we had really fresh beats and songs kids could sing along with when they heard them the first time. We were teen-agers; you wouldn't expect us to sing . . . like Mahalia Jackson sang in 1940."[72]

Toni Braxton sings at the Essence Music Festival in Houston, Texas, in 2006.

Refusing to Stay Put

Meanwhile, the many other styles that have developed from the wellspring of black popular music continue to flourish. For example, traditional blues and R&B enjoy vibrant scenes, with many active performers and enthusiastic audiences. Among the many prominent examples are Irma Thomas, the smoky-voiced Queen of New Orleans R&B; traditionally minded acoustic bluesman Keb' Mo'; soul legend Solomon Burke; and Robert Cray, an R&B- and blues-influenced guitarist, songwriter, and singer.

Jazz has enjoyed periodic surges in popularity over the decades, though it has never achieved the massive audience it had during the swing years. The music has gone through a number of phases over the decades. It has combined with funk, merged with rock, and passed through a period of free jazz, in which traditional concepts like meter, chord changes, and melody were stripped away.

More recently, there has been a fad for smooth jazz, essentially an easy-listening style that emphasizes setting a mellow mood. There has also been a movement to return to the timeless elements of swing and bebop. The most influential figure in this back-to-basics movement has been trumpeter Wynton Marsalis.

Trumpeter Wynton Marsalis is dedicated to keeping the sounds of jazz alive for future generations.

Marsalis, part of a prominent New Orleans musical family, was the first person of any race to win Grammy Awards in both jazz and classical music on the same night. In his role as a champion of classic jazz, Marsalis has been key in establishing a repertory ensemble based in New York City's Lincoln Center, dedicated to keeping alive the music of composers such as Duke Ellington. Marsalis's efforts have inspired similar groups all around the country.

Overall—taking into account jazz, hip-hop, blues, R&B, soul, and all the rest—black popular music has amassed a deep and abundant legacy in a history spanning more than a century. It has so much history, in fact, that a number of museums around the country are dedicated to celebrating various aspects of it. One of the most ambitious of these is still in the planning stages: a Smithsonian-affiliated Museum of African-American Music in Newark, New Jersey.

But black music, of course, is not just something to be displayed in a museum, frozen in time. It is an ever-changing genre that is very much alive, growing and evolving as public taste changes and new experiments catch on. Writer Gerri Hirshey notes, "Black American music just won't stay put."[73] It will no doubt refuse to stay put for a long time to come.

Notes

Introduction: A Hundred Years— and More—of Music

1. Quoted in Eileen Southern, *The Music of Black Americans: A History*. New York: Norton, 1997, p. 575.
2. Quoted in Gerri Hirshey, *Nowhere to Run: The Story of Soul Music*. New York: Times, 1984, p. xiii.
3. Quoted in Ted Fox, *Showtime at the Apollo*. New York: Da Capo, 1993, p. 82.

Chapter 1: The Roots of Black Music

4. Robert Darden, *People Get Ready! A New History of Black Gospel Music*. New York: Continuum, 2004, p. 1.
5. Southern, *The Music of Black Americans*, p. 5.
6. Quoted in Southern, *The Music of Black Americans*, p. 48.
7. Quoted in Southern, *The Music of Black Americans*, p. 84.
8. James Weldon Johnson, "Negro Folk Songs and Spirituals," Document Records, Vintage Blues, Jazz, and Afro-American Music CDs for Sale. www.document-records.com/index.asp?content=http://www.document-records.com/content_show_article.asp?id=189&offset=90.
9. Quoted in *Popular Songs in American History*, "The Drinking Gourd." www.contemplator.com/america/gourd.html.
10. Southern, *The Music of Black Americans*, p. 92.
11. Thomas L. Morgan and William Barlow, *From Cakewalks to Concert Halls: An Illustrated History of African American Popular Music from 1895 to 1930*. Washington, DC: Elliott and Clark, 1992, p. 12.
12. Julius Lester, *Black Folktales*. New York: Grove Weidenfeld, 1969, p. 113.
13. Horace Clarence Boyer, *The Golden Age of Gospel*. Urbana and Chicago: University of Illinois Press, 2000, p. 19.

Chapter 2: Early Ragtime, Blues, and Jazz

14. David A. Jasen and Gene Jones, *That American Rag: The Story of Ragtime from Coast to Coast*. New York: Schirmer, 2000, p. xxiv.
15. Quoted in Mark Anthony Neal, *What the Music Said: Black Popular Music and Black Popular Culture*. New York: Routledge, 1999, p. 8.
16. Southern, *The Music of Black Americans*, p. 317.
17. Quoted in Thinkexist.com, "The Blues Quotes and Quotations." http://en.thinkexist.com/quotes/with/keyword/the_blues/2.html.
18. Quoted in Viv Broughton, *Black Gospel: An Illustrated History of the Gospel Sound*. Poole, UK: Blandford, 1985, p. 32.

19. Quoted in Southern, *The Music of Black Americans*, p. 332.

20. Morgan and Barlow, *From Cakewalks to Concert Halls,* p. 33.

21. Quoted in Albert McCarthy, *Louis Armstrong.* 1959. Reprint, New York: A.S. Barnes, 1961, p. 26.

22. Jasen and Jones, *That American Rag,* p. xxxvii.

23. Quoted in Morgan and Barlow, *From Cakewalks to Concert Halls*, p. 68.

24. Arthur Kempton, *Boogaloo: The Quintessence of American Popular Music.* New York: Pantheon, 2003, p. 21.

Chapter 3: From Swing to Bebop

25. Quoted in John Edward Hasse, *Beyond Category: The Life and Genius of Duke Ellington.* New York: Simon and Schuster, 1993, p. 404.

26. Whitney Balliett, "Celebrating the Duke," *New Yorker*: November 29, 1993, p. 136.

27. Southern, *The Music of Black Americans*, p. 391.

28. Quoted in Guthrie P. Ramsey Jr., *Race Music: Black Cultures from Bebop to Hip-Hop.* Berkeley and Los Angeles: University of California Press, 2003, p. 96.

29. Dizzy Gillespie and Al Frazer, *To Be or Not to Bop.* Garden City, NY: Doubleday, 1979, p. 201.

30. Quoted in Fox, *Showtime at the Apollo,* p. 137.

31. Pete Welding, "Muddy Waters," The Official Muddy Waters Website—Biography. www.muddywaters.com/bio.html.

32. William Barlow and Cheryl Finley, *From Swing to Soul: An Illustrated Histo-ry of African American Popular Music from 1930 to 1960.* Washington, DC: Elliott and Clark, 1994, p. 82.

Chapter 4: R&B and Rock and Roll

33. Quoted in Fox, *Showtime at the Apollo,* p. 170.

34. Quoted in Hirshey, *Nowhere to Run,* p. 23.

35. Ramsey, *Race Music,* p. 64.

36. Quoted in Rolling Stone, eds., *The Rolling Stone Interviews, 1967–80.* New York: Rolling Stone, 1981, p. 224.

37. Quoted in Anthony DeCurtis and James Heinke, eds., *The Rolling Stone History of Rock & Roll.* New York: Random House/Rolling Stone, 1992, p. 51.

38. Hirshey, *Nowhere to Run*, p. 59.

Chapter 5: That Sweet Soul Music

39. Quoted in Hirshey, *Nowhere to Run,* p. 315.

40. Quoted in DeCurtis and Heinke, *The Rolling Stone History of Rock & Roll*, pp. 260–61.

41. Quoted in Darden, *People Get Ready!* p. 245.

42. Whitney Balliett, *American Singers: 27 Portraits in Song.* New York: Oxford University Press, 1988, p. 57.

43. Quoted in Jon Pareles and Bernard Weinraub, "Ray Charles, Bluesy Essence of Soul, Is Dead at 73," *New York Times,* June 11, 2004, p. A1.

44. Quoted in Broughton, *Black Gospel,* p. 114.

45. Quoted in Hirshey, *Nowhere to Run,* p. 47.

46. Quoted in Anthony Heilbut, *The Gospel*

Sound: Good News and Bad Times. New York: Limelight, 1997, p. 277.

47. Peter Guralnick, *Sweet Soul Music: Rhythm and Blues and the Southern Dream of Freedom*. New York: Little, Brown, 1999, p. 332.

48. Quoted in Patricia Romanowski and Holly George-Warren, eds., *The New Rolling Stone Encyclopedia of Rock & Roll*. New York: Rolling Stone, 1995, p. 839.

49. Quoted in Rolling Stone, *The Rolling Stone Interviews, 1967–80*, p. 71.

50. Kempton, *Boogaloo*, p. 216.

51. Quoted in DeCurtis and Heinke, *The Rolling Stone History of Rock & Roll*, pp. 275–76.

52. Quoted in Hirshey, *Nowhere to Run*, p. 73.

Chapter 6: Dancing the Seventies Away

53. Quoted in DeCurtis and Heinke, *The Rolling Stone History of Rock & Roll*, p. 418.

54. Robert Palmer, *Rock and Roll: An Unruly History*. New York: Harmony, 1995, p. 249.

55. Quoted in Ramsey, *Race Music*, p. 2.

56. Quoted in Broughton, *Black Gospel*, p. 125.

57. Kevin Phinney, *Souled American: How Black Music Transformed White Culture*. New York: Billboard, 2005, p. 249.

58. Neal, *What the Music Said*, p. 103.

59. Mikal Gilmore, *Night Beat*. New York: Doubleday, 1998, p. 242.

60. Quoted in Ed Ward, Geoffrey Stokes, and Ken Tucker, *Rock of Ages: The Rolling Stone History of Rock & Roll*. New York: Rolling Stone, 1986, p. 533.

61. Quoted in DeCurtis and Heinke, *The Rolling Stone History of Rock & Roll*, p. 523.

62. Neal, *What the Music Said*, p. 103.

Chapter 7: The Beats Go On

63. Quoted in Chris Bruce and Adam Woog, eds., *Crossroads: The Experience Music Project Collection*. Seattle: EMP, 2000, p. 156.

64. Quoted in Jim Fricke and Charlie Ahern, *Yes, Yes, Y'all: The Experience Music Project Oral History of Hip-Hop's First Decade*. New York: Da Capo, 2002, p. i.

65. Quoted in Bruce and Woog, *Crossroads*, pp. 153–54.

66. Neal, *What the Music Said*, p. 138.

67. Quoted in Kempton, *Boogaloo*, 2003, p. 441.

68. Quoted in Jim Fricke and Charlie Ahern, *Yes, Yes, Y'all*, p. ii.

69. Quoted in Jared Green, ed., *Rap and Hip-Hop*. San Diego: Greenhaven, 2003, p. 90.

70. Quoted in Tika Milan, "The Roots' New Album: Heavy But No Debbie Downer," *Rolling Stone*, June 21, 2006. www.rollingstone.com/news/story/10 617577/the_roots_new_album_heavy _but_no_debbie_downer.

71. Paul Friedlander, *Rock and Roll: A Social History*. New York: Westview/ HarperCollins, 1996, p. 269.

72. Quoted in Darden, *People Get Ready!* p. 313.

73. Hirshey, *Nowhere to Run*, p. xv.

Chronology

1619
Slaves first arrive in North America, bringing African music.

1600s–1800s
Spirituals develop as a form of African American folk music.

1800s
Minstrel shows are popular.

1865
Slavery ends.

1871
The Fisk Jubilee Singers are formed.

late 1800s–early 1900s
Blues, ragtime, and jazz develop; gospel music develops from spirituals.

1920s
Black musical theater and vaudeville flourish; sales of recordings by black popular artists skyrocket.

1930s–mid-1940s
Swing develops.

late 1940s
Bebop develops as swing recedes in popularity; electric blues develops; LP records create new venues of expression for musicians.

late 1940s–mid-1950s
Rhythm and blues (R&B) develops; rock and roll evolves out of R&B.

late 1950s–late-1960s
Soul develops out of R&B; the British Invasion inspires renewed American interest in blues.

1970s
Funk and disco emerge.

1980s
Hip-hop and rap develop; Michael Jackson emerges as a solo artist.

1990s–present
Rap continues to evolve; new forms of R&B also continue to develop.

For Further Reading

Books

William Barlow and Cheryl Finley, *From Swing to Soul: An Illustrated History of African American Popular Music from 1930 to 1960*. Washington, DC: Elliott and Clark, 1994. This continuation of Barlow's excellent history, begun in *From Cakewalks to Concert Halls*, is frustratingly organized but well illustrated.

Jim Fricke and Charlie Ahern, *Yes, Yes, Y'all: The Experience Music Project Oral History of Hip-Hop's First Decade*. New York: Da Capo, 2002. An interesting oral history of early hip-hop, told through the words of its pioneers and heavily illustrated with photos, reproductions of flyers, and other material.

Jared Green, ed., *Rap and Hip Hop*. San Diego: Greenhaven, 2003. A well-chosen selection of excerpts from writings about the music.

Peter Guralnick, *Sweet Soul Music: Rhythm and Blues and the Southern Dream of Freedom*. New York: Little, Brown, 1999. A reprint of a 1986 classic by a distinguished writer on American roots music.

James Haskins, *Black Music in America*. New York: HarperCollins, 1987. A simply written text by a professor of English who specializes in African American music.

Thomas L. Morgan and William Barlow, *From Cakewalks to Concert Halls: An Illustrated History of African American Popular Music from 1895 to 1930*. Washington, DC: Elliott and Clark, 1992. A beautifully illustrated and clearly written short history, with dozens of terrific reproductions of sheet-music covers and other representative graphics from the era.

Web Sites

EMPlive.org (www.emplive.org). This site, maintained by the Experience Music Project museum in Seattle, covers many aspects of American pop, including black music, and is a fascinating source of fun and informative material.

The Blue Highway (www.thebluehigh way.com/). This site, maintained by a fan, is another excellent source for information about the blues.

Blues Foundation (www.blues.org/index. php4). The Web site of an important foundation dedicated to promoting and preserving the blues.

Jazz Roots—Early Jazz History on JASS.COM (www.jass.com/). An extremely thorough site on the early history and figures of jazz.

Negrospirituals.com (www.negrospirituals. com/). This site provides a good capsule history of the music and biographies of important figures in gospel music.

Index

Picture Credits

Cover: Getty Images
AP Photos, 40, 46, 85, 94, 95
© Bettmann/CORBIS, 20, 30, 37, 50, 56, 62, 63, 80
© Christian Simonpietri/SYGMA/CORBIS, 68
© CORBIS, 90
Getty Images, 87, 91
© Henry Diltz/CORBIS, 7
Hulton Archive/Getty Images, 19, 23, 24, 27, 32, 36, 41,
    48, 52, 58, 73, 74, 75, 77
© James L. Amos/CORBIS, 79
© Jeff Albertson/CORBIS, 65
© Lynn Goldsmith/CORBIS, 82, 93
© Mosaic Images/CORBIS, 44
North Wind Pictures, 11, 14
Time & Life Pictures/Getty Images, 55
© Tony Frank/SYGMA/CORBIS, 70
© Underwood & Underwood/CORBIS, 39

About the Author

Adam Woog has written more than fifty books for adults, teens, and children. For Lucent Books, he has explored such subjects as Louis Armstrong, Prohibition, Anne Frank, Elvis Presley, Ray Charles, gospel music, folk music, sweatshops, and the New Deal. Woog lives with his wife and their daughter in Seattle, Washington.